Operation Research

Prof (Dr.) D.N. Mishra
Director Management
Saroj Institute of Technology and Management,
Lucknow (UP) India

Prof. S.K.Agarwal
Professor (Electronics & Communication)
Saroj Institute of Technology and Management,
Lucknow (UP) India

Pooja Sinha
Senior Lecturer
Department of Management
Saroj Institute of Technology and Management,
Lucknow (UP) India

Lucknow

Published by
word-press
(Publishing Division)
Khushnuma Complex Basement
7, Meerabai Marg (Behind Jawahar Bhawan)
Lucknow 226 001 U.P. (INDIA)
Tel. : 91-522-2209542, 2209543, 2209544, 2209545
Fax : 0522-4045308
E-Mail : ibdco@airtelmail.in

First Edition 2009

Price: Rs. 160/-

ISBN 978-93-80257-01-3

Composed & Designed at :

Panacea Computers
2nd Floor, Agarwal Sabha Bhawan, Subhash Mohal
Sadar Cantt., Lucknow-226 002
Phone : 0522-2483312, 9335927082, 9452295008
E-mail : prasgupt@rediffmail.com

Printed at:

Salasar Imaging Systems
C-7/5, Lawrence Road Industrial Area
Delhi - 110 035
Tel. : 011-27185653, 9810064311

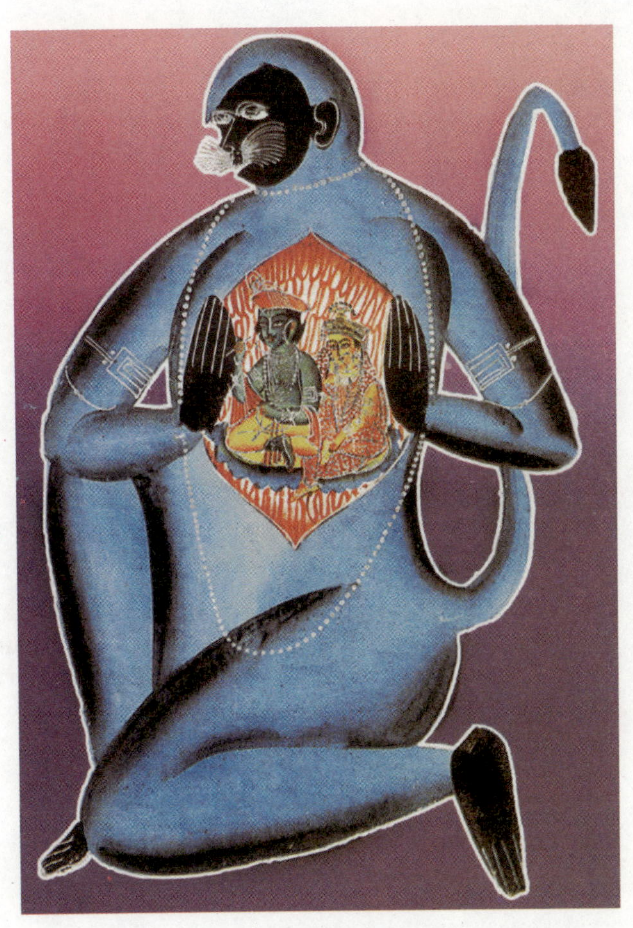

Dedicated to
Shri Hanuman Ji

Preface

In a competitive business environment, it has become essential for the prosperity and growth in the field of operation research. The growing importance of new techniques has been emphasized the need for developing Operation to Research models to provide practical utility. These OR models which constitute the subject matters to develop in readers an understanding of problem solving methods.

Each chapter begins with important and interesting examples from various fields. This book will be of immense use for all those who want to learn how to analyze OR situation to arrive at optimum decision. This should be of equal interest to students' professionals and the interested readers.

Every effort has been made to present the subject matter in easy, clear and systematic manner. This book will be useful for the student of M.Com, C.A., PGDBM and M.B.A. who need both theoretical and practical knowledge of operation research techniques.

We would like to thank the publisher for the efficient and thoroughly professional way in which the whole task was complete. We sincerely thank Shri Kaptan Singh for his valuable suggestions. We also thank our family members for their constant encouragement for writing this book.

We invite the reader to offer their valuable suggestion.

CONTENTS

Chapter **1**

General Concept of Operation Research

Course Outline

1.1 Introduction:

(The Historical Development of O.R.)

The main origin of O.R was during world –war II; At that time Britain was having very limited military resources, therefore there was an urgent need to allocate resources to the various military operations, and to the activities with in each operations in an effective manner. Therefore, the British military executives and managers called upon a team of scientists to apply a scientific approach to study the strategic and tactical problems related to air and land defense of the country. The work of this team was named as O.R. in Britain. The success of O.R. in military, attracted attention of industrial management in the new field.

Now a day, the impact of O.R. can be seen in many areas. A large number of Management consulting firms are currently engaged in O.R. activities, these activities include transportation system, Libraries, hospitals, city planning, financial institution etc. Many Business and Organizations problem can be solved by using O.R techniques. With the help of O.R. techniques, we may not get the best answers but definitely we are able to find the bad answers where worse exist. Thus O.R. techniques are always able to save us from worse situations of practical life.

1.2 The Nature and Definition of O.R. :

There are many opinions related to the definition of O.R. which is given below.

"OR is a scientific method of providing executive departments with a quantitative basis for decisions regarding the operations under their control".

– – – Morse and Kimbal (1946)

"OR is the scientific method of providing executive with an analytical and objective basis for decisions".

– – – – P.M.S. Blackett (1948)

"O.R. is the art of giving bad answer to problems to which otherwise worse answer are given".

– – – T.L. Saaty (1958)

"O.R. is scientific approach to problem solving for executive management".

– – C. Kittee

"O.R. is systematic method oriented study of the basic structures, characteristics, functions and relationships of an organization to provide the executive with a sound, scientific and quantitative basis for decision making". **– – –E.L. Arnoff & M.J. Netzorg**

1.3 Characteristics of O.R.

(1) System Orientation of O.R.

One of the most important characteristics of OR study is its concerned with problems as a whole or its system orientation. This means that an activity by any part of an organization has some effect on the activity of every part. Therefore, to evaluate any decision, one must identify all possible interactions and determine their impact on the organization as a whole.

(2) The use of Interdisciplinary team

The second characteristic of OR study is that it is performed by a team of scientists whose individuals members have been drawn from different scientific and engineering disciplines. For example, one may find a mathematician, statistician, physicist, psychologist, economist and engineering working together on an OR problem.

(3) Application of Scientific Method

Sometime, we have to use the scientific method for solving the problem of OR. It is not related to laboratories experiment like physics and chemistry but it is related to the real life experiment. For example, no company can risk its failure in order to conduct a successful experiment. Though, experimentations on sub system is some times resorted to, by and large, a research approach that does not involve experimentation on the total system is preferred.

(3) Uncovering of New Problems

OR problem may uncover a number of new problems. Of course, all these uncovered problems need not be solved at the same time. However, in order to derive maximum benefit, each one of them must be solved.

(4) Quantitative Solutions

It provides the management with a quantitative basis for decision making.

(5) Human factor

Human factor is an important component of the OR study. Without human factor OR study is incomplete.

1.4 Phases of OR:

OR study generally involves the following phases

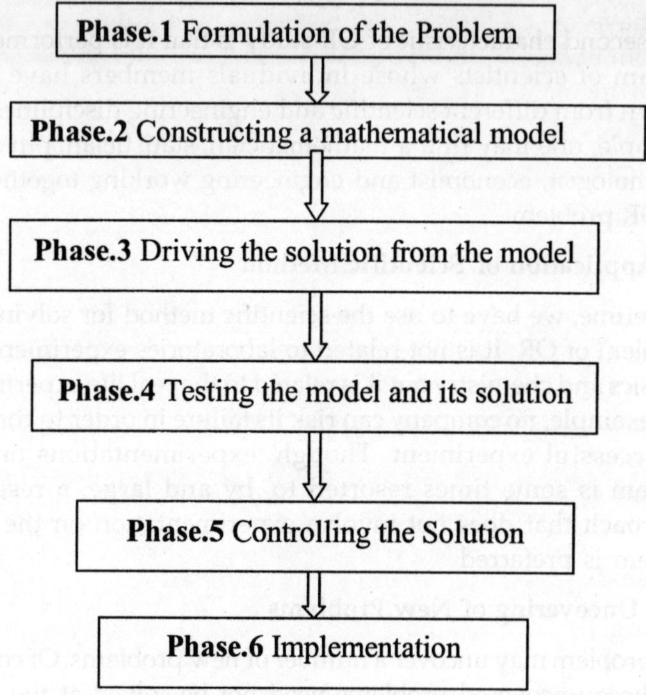

Phase 1. Formulation of the Problem:

To find the solution of the OR problem, we must have to formulate the problem in the form of an appropriate model. The following information will be required for this.

(1) Decision Maker

(2) Objective

(3) Controllable Factor (Variable)

(4) Uncontrollable Factor (Variable)

(5) Restrictions or Constraints

Phase 2. Constructing a mathematical model

The second phase is concerned with the reformulation of the problem in an appropriate form which is convenient for analysis; we have to construct a mathematical model representing the system under study. A mathematical model should include the following three important basic factors.

(i) Decision Variables

(ii) Constraints

(iii) Objective function

Phase 3. Driving the solution from the model

In this phase, we will have to compute the above problem by using OR tools or techniques and we will get the solutions. After formulating the mathematical model for the problem under consideration, the next phase is to derive a solution from this model. Here in Operation Research we always in the search for an optimal solution. An optimal solution is one which maximize or minimize the objective function in the model.

Phase 4. Testing the model and its solution

After getting the solution, it is necessary to test the solution for errors if any. This may be done by re-examining the formulation of the problem and comparing it with the model that may help to reveal any mistakes.

Phase 5. Controlling the solution

This phase establishes controls over the solution with any degree of satisfaction. The model requires immediate modification as soon as the controlled variables (one or more) change significantly, otherwise the model goes out of control. As the conditions are constantly changing in the world, the model and the solution may not remain valid for a long time.

Phase 6. Implementation

The final phase of an OR study is to implement the optimum solution derived by the OR team. As the conditions are constantly changing in the world, the model and the solution may not remain valid for a long time. Therefore, as the change occurs, it is to be detected as soon as possible so that the model, its solution and the resulting course of action can be modified accordingly.

1.5 Quantitative techniques of OR

Operation research, as its name suggests, gives stress on analysis of operations as a whole. For this purpose, it uses any suitable techniques or tools available from the fields of mathematics, statistics, cost analysis or numerical calculations. Some such techniques are listed below.

(1) Linear programming
(2) Non - linear programming
(3) Integer Programming
(4) Dynamic Programming
(5) Goal Programming
(6) Game theory
(7) Inventory Control
(8) PERT-CPM
(9) Simulation
(10) Queuing theory

1.6 Scope of Operations Research

1. In Industry:-

OR has been successfully applied in industry in the fields of production, blending product mix, inventory control, demand forecast, sale and purchase, transportation, repair and maintenance, scheduling sequencing, planning and control of projects etc.

2. In Defence:-

OR has a wide scope for application in defense operations. All the defense operations are carried out by a different agencies, namely airforce, army and navy. Operation research helpful for achieving the desired goals of different agencies.

3. In planning:-

OR is helpful for planning of various activities of the organization. Planning is the important function of management. Without effective planning, we can not achieve the desired goals.

4. In Agriculture:-

OR approach needs to be equally developed in agriculture sector on national or international basis. Every country is facing the problem of optimum allocation of land to various crops in accordance with the climatic conditions and optimum distributions of water from various resources like canal for irrigation purposes. Thus, there is a need of determining best policies under the prescribed restrictions.

5. In Public Utilities:-

OR approach is directly applicable to business and society. It is also equally applicable for big and small organization. It is helpful for deciding the premium rates of various L.I.C policies. It has also been extensively used in petroleum, paper chemical, metal processing, aircraft, rubber, transport and distribution, mining and textile industries.

1.7 Model in Operation Research:

When we represent a real life situation in some abstract form whether physical or mathematical, bringing out the relationships of its important ingredients, we call it as model. Thus, model need not described all the aspects of this situation, but it should signify and identify important factors and their inter-relationships to describe the total situation.

There are number of models used in OR. Some of the basic types are described below.

(1) Physical Models: These models provide a physical appearance of the real object under the study of either reduced in size or scaled up. Physical models are useful only in design problems because they are easy to observe, build and describe. Physical models are classified into the following two categories.

(i) Iconic Models: Iconic models represents the system as it is but in different size. Thus, Iconic models are obtained by enlarging or reducing the size of the system. In other words, they are images. Examples of iconic models are blueprints of a home, maps, globes, photographs, drawings, airplanes, trains, etc.

(ii) Analog Models: These models do not look like the real situation but represent and behave like a system under study. For example, the organization chart represents the structure, authority and responsibilities relationship with boxes and arrows: and maps in different colors represent water, desert and other geographical features.

(2) Symbolic Models: These models use symbols (letters, numbers) and functions to represent variables and their relationship to describe the properties of the system. These models are also used to represent relationships which can be represented in a physical form. Symbolic models can be classified into two categories.

(i) Verbal Models: These models describe a situation in written or spoken language.

Written sentences, books, etc. are examples of verbal model.

(ii) Mathematical Models: These models involve the use of mathematical Symbols, letters, numbers and mathematical operators (+, - , ÷ ,×) to represent relationships among various variables of the system to describe its properties or behavior.

(3) Heuristic Models: These models use intuitive rules or guidelines to solve a particular problem. These models are not based on any definite mathematical expression or relationships, but problem solving based on past experience or approach formulated on the basis of definite stepped procedure. These models need an ample amount of creativity and experience by the decision maker.

1.8 Advantages and Limitation of Operation Research:

Operation research is useful for improving quality of managerial decision making. By using various tools and techniques of OR we can get optimal solution of the problem. However, besides certain advantages, OR approach has some limitations. There are some advantages and limitations are given below.

Advantages:

(1.) It compels the decision-maker to be quite explicit about his objective, assumptions and his perspective to constraints.

(2.) It makes the decision-maker to very carefully about what variables influence the decisions.

(3.) Quickly points out gaps in the data required to support workable solutions to a problem.

(4.) Its models can be solved by a computer, thus the management can get enough time for decisions that require quantitative approach.

Limitations:

(1) Often solution to a problem is derived either by making it simplified or simplifying assumptions and thus, such solutions have limitations.

(2) Sometimes models do not represent the realistic situations in which decisions must be made.

(3) Often decision-maker is not fully aware of the limitations of the models that he is using.

(4) Many 'real world' problems just cannot have an OR solution.

1.9 Applications of Operations Research:

Some of the industrial/ government/business problems which can be analyzed by OR approach have been arranged by functional areas as follows.

- Finance and Accounting
- Marketing
- Purchasing, Procurement and Exploration
- Production Management
- Personnel Management
- Techniques and General Management

- Government

1.10 Practice Problem

(1) What is Operation Research?

(2) What is OR? Give a brief historical development of OR.

(3) Discuss Various Phases in solving an OR problem.

(4) Discuss scientific method in OR.

(5) Define OR and discuss its scope.

(6) Discuss the three types of models with special emphasis on their important logical properties and their relationship with to each other.

(7) What are the advantage and disadvantage of Operation research models?

(8) Discuss the advantages and limitations of using results from a mathematical model to make decision about operations.

(9) Define OR. Give the main characteristics of OR. Also discuss the importance of OR in Decision-making.

(10) Explain the general nature of optimization problems and discuss their significance in relation to OR problems.

(10) Explain the applications of OR.

(11) Describe the situations where OR techniques can be used.

(12) Give any three useful definitions of Operations Research and explain them.

Objective Question:

1. Operation Research is
   (a) Multi-disciplinary
   (b) Scientific
   (c) Intuitive
   (d) All of the above

2. Operation Research analyst do not
   (a) Predict future operations
   (b) Built more than one model
   (c) Collect relevant data

(d) Recommended decision and accept

3. A model is
   (a) An essence of reality
   (b) An approximation
   (c) An idealization
   (d) All of the above

4. Managerial decision are based on
   (a) An evaluation of quantitative data
   (b) The use of quantitative factors
   (c) Numbers produced by formal models
   (d) All of the above

5. A physical model is example of
   (a) An iconic model
   (b) An analogue model
   (c) A verbal model
   (d) A mathematical model

6. Every mathematical model
   (a) Must be deterministic
   (b) Requires computer aid for its solution
   (c) Represents data in numerical form
   (d) All of the above

7. OR approach is typically based on the use of
   (a) Physical model
   (b) Mathematical model
   (c) Iconic model
   (d) Descriptive model

8. The qualitative approach to decision analysis relies on
   (a) Experience
   (b) Judgment
   (c) Intuition
   (d) All of the above

9. An optimization model
   (a) Mathematically provides the best decision
   (b) Provides decision within its limited context.

(c) Helps in evaluating various alternatives constantly.
(d) All of the above.

10. Operation research practishioners do not
(a) Take responsibility for solution implementation.
(b) Collect essential data.
(c) Predict future actions/operations
(d) Build more than one model.

Answer: 1 (a), 2 (a), 3 (d), 4 (d) , 5 (a) , 6 (c) , 7 (b), 8 (d), 9 (d), 10 (d).

Chapter 2

Linear Programming Problem

Course outline

2.1 Introduction:

Linear programming comes under the allocation problem. A problem which involves the allocation of given number of resources to the job is called an allocation problem. The objective of these problems is to optimize the total effectiveness i.e to minimize the total cost or maximize the total return. Generally, there are three types of allocation problems :

(1) Linear programming problem

(2) Transportation problem

(3) Assignment Problem

We shall discuss the assignment problem and the transportation problem in the next chapter of this book.

2.2 Linear Programming Problem

The term Linear Programming is the combination of the two term **'Linear'** and **'Programming'**. The term **'linear'** means that all the relations in the particular problem are linear and the term **'programming'** refers to the process determining particular programme or plan of action.

The linear programming method is a technique of choosing the best alternative from the set of feasible alternatives, in the situations in which the objective functions as well as constraints can be expressed as linear mathematical function.

The linear function which is to be optimized is called the **objective function** and the conditions of the problem expressed as simultaneous linear equations (or inequalities) are referred as **constraints.**

2.3 Mathematical Formulation of a L.P.P.

A general linear programming problem can be stated as follows:

Find $X_1, X_2, X_3, \ldots\ldots X_n$. which optimize the linear function.

$Z = C_1X_1 + C_2X_2 + \ldots\ldots + C_nX_n$ ....(1)

Subject to the constraints

$A_{11}X_1 + A_{12}X_2 + \ldots\ldots + A_{1j}X_j + \ldots\ldots A_{1n}X_n \ (\leq = \geq)\ b_1$

$A_{21}X_1 + A_{22}X_2 + \ldots\ldots + A_{2j}X_j + \ldots\ldots A_{2n}X_n \ (\leq = \geq)\ b_2$

....

....

$A_{i1}X_1 + A_{i2}X_2 + \ldots\ldots + A_{ij}X_j + \ldots\ldots A_{in}X_n \ (\leq = \geq)\ b_i$

....

$A_{m1}X_1 + A_{m2}X_2 + \ldots\ldots + A_{mi}X_j + \ldots\ldots A_{mn}X_n \ (\leq = \geq) b_n$

and non-negative restrictions

$$X_j \geq 0,\ j=1,2,3 \ldots\ldots n.$$

Where all A_{ij}'s , b_i's and c_j's are constants and X_j's are variables.

2.4 Matrix form of LP problem

The LPP can be expressed in the form of matrix as follows.

Maximize or Minimize Z =CX is the objective function.

Subject to

AX $(\leq = \geq)$ b constraints equation, $b > 0$, $X \geq 0$ Non-Negativity restrictions.

Where $X = (X_1, X_2, \ldots\ldots\ldots X_n)$

$C = (C_1, C_2, \ldots\ldots\ldots C_n)$

$$b = \begin{pmatrix} b_1 \\ b_2 \\ \cdot \\ \cdot \\ \cdot \\ b_m \end{pmatrix} \qquad A = \begin{pmatrix} a_{11} & a_{12} & \ldots\ldots & a_{1n} \\ a_{21} & a_{22} & \ldots\ldots & a_{2n} \\ \cdot & & & \\ \cdot & & & \\ \cdot & & & \\ a_{m1} & a_{m2} & \ldots\ldots & a_{mn} \end{pmatrix}$$

2.5 Procedure for formulation of L.P. problems

Step 1. To write down the decision variables of the problem.

Step 2. To formulate the objective function to be optimized (Maximized or Minimized) as a linear function of the decision variable.

Step 3. To formulate the other conditions of the problem such as resource limitation, market constraints, interrelations between variables etc, as linear equations or equations in terms of decision variables.

Step 4. To add Non-negativity constraints from the considerations so that the negative values of the decision variables do not have any valid physical interpretation.

The objective function, the set of constraints and the Non-negative constraints together form a linear programming problem.

Example 1. A company manufactures 3 products A, B and C. The profit are Rs 3, Rs 2 and Rs 4 respectively. The company has two machines and given below is the required processing time in minutes for each machine on each product.

Machines	Products		
	A	B	C
I	4	3	2

II	2	2	4

Machines I and II have 2000 and 2500 minutes respectively. The company must manufacture 100A's , 200 B's and 50 C's but no more than 150 A's. Find the number of units of each product to be manufactured by the company to maximize the profit. Formulate the above as a L.P model.

Solutions: Formulation of the Mathematical model of the problem

Decision Variables:

Let $X_{1,}$ X_2 and X_3 be the number of units of each product to be manufactured by the company to maximize the profit.

Objective functions:

Since the profit for the products are given, we have to maximize the profit then

$$\text{Max (Z)} = 3X_1+2X_2+4X_3$$

Constraints:

There are two machines and each machine have limited time which are 2000 minutes for machine I and 2500 minutes for machine II then the total required processing time for each machine are restricted.

$$4X_1+3X_2+5X_3 \leq 2000$$

$$2X_1+2X_2+4X_3 \leq 2500$$

And the condition is also applied for the quantity to be manufactured by the company.

$$100 \leq X_1 \leq 150$$

$$200 \leq X_2$$

$$50 \leq X_3$$

Finally the complete L.P.P is

$$\text{Max } (Z) = 3X_1 + 2X_2 + 4X_3$$

Subject to

$$4X_1 + 3X_2 + 5X_3 \le 2000$$
$$2X_1 + 2X_2 + 4X_3 \le 2500$$
$$100 \le X_1 \le 150$$
$$200 \le X_2$$
$$50 \le X_3$$
$$X_1, X_2, X_3 \le 0$$

Example.2 A resourceful home decorator manufactures two types of lamps says A and B. Both Lamps go through two technician's first a cutter, second a finisher. Lamp A requires 2 hrs of the cutter's time and 1hrs of the finisher's time. Lamp B requires 1 hrs of cutter's time and 2 hrs of finisher's time. The cutter has 104 hrs and finisher has 76 hrs of available time each month. Profit per lamp A is Rs 6 and per B lamp is Rs 11. Assuming that he can sale all that he produces, how many of each type of lamps should be manufactured to obtain the best return.

Solution: Formulation of the Mathematical model of the problem

For clear understanding of the problem, first we have to construct a table.

Lamps	Cutter	Finisher	Profit
A	2 hrs	1hrs	Rs 6
B	1hrs	2hrs	Rs 11
Available time	104 hrs	76hrs	

Decision Variables:

Let the decorator manufacture X_1 and X_2 lamps of type A and B respectively.

Objective Function:

Therefore, the total profit (in Rs.) has to be maximized.

$Max(z)=6X_1+11X_2$

Constraints:

The manufacturer has limited time for manufacturing the lamp. There are 104 hrs available for cutting and 76 hrs available for finishing.

Thus, total processing time is restricted.

$2X_1+X_2 \leq 104$

$X_1+X_2 \leq 76$

Finally the complete L.P.P. is $Max(z)=6X_1+11X_2$

Subject to

$2X_1+X_2 \leq 104$

$X_1+X_2 \leq 76$

And $X_1 X_2 \leq 0$

2.6 Some Important Definitions in LPP:

1. A set of values X_1, X_2......Xn which satisfies the constraints (2) of the LPP is called its solution.
2. Any solution to a LPP which satisfies the non-negativity restrictions (3) of the LPP is called its feasible solution.
3. Any feasible solution which optimizes (minimizes or maximizes) the objective function (1) of the LPP is called its optimum solution.
4. Given a system of m linear equations with n variables (m<n), any solution which is obtained by solving for m variables keeping the remaining n-m variables zero is called a basic solution. Such m variables are called basic variables and the remaining variables are called non basic variables.
5. A basic feasible solution is a basic solution which also satisfies (3), that is all basic variables are non- negative.

Basic feasible solutions are of two types:

(a) **Non-degenerate:** A non degenerate basic feasible solution is the basic feasible solution which has exactly m positive X_i (i=1,2..........m) i.e. None of the basic variables are zero.

(b) Degenerate: A basic feasible solution is said to degenerate if one or more basic variables are zero.

6. If the value of the objective function z can be increased or decreased indefinitely, such solution are called **unbounded solutions.**

2.7 Standard form of an LP Problem

We have to convert the LP problem into the standard form of LP before the use of simplex method.

The standard form of the LP problem should have the following characteristics :

(i) All the constraints should be expressed as equations by adding **slack** or **surplus** and / or **artificial** variables.

(ii) The right hand side of each constraints should be made non negative if it is not, this should be done by multiplying both sides of the resulting constraints by -1.

(iii) The objective function should be of the maximization type.

The general standard form of the LP problem is expressed as:

Optimize (Max or Min)Z =
$C_1X_1+C_2X_2+......+C_nX_n+0.S_1+0.S_2+.........0.S_m$

Subject to the linear constraints

$A_{11}X_1+ A_{12}X_2+..........+A_{1j}X_j+......A_{1n}X_n + S_1 = b_1$

$A_{21}X_1+A_{22}X_2+..........+A_{2j}X_j+.......A_{2n}X_n + S_2 = b_2$

....

....

$A_{i1}X_1+A_{i2}X_2+.........+A_{ij}X_j+.........A_{in}X_n + S_n = b_i$

....

$A_{m1}X_1+A_{m2}X_2+........+A_{mj}X_j+........A_{mn}X_n + S_m = b_m$

And $X_1, X_2, \ldots\ldots\ldots\ldots, X_n, S_1, S_2, \ldots\ldots\ldots\ldots S_m \geq 0$

Definitions of Slack, Surplus and Artificial variables

(1) If the constrains of a general LPP be

$$\sum_{j=1}^{n} a_{ij} X_i \leq b_i \ (i = 1, 2 \ldots\ldots m)$$

then the non-negative variables S_i which are introduced to convert the inequalities (≤) to the equalities.

$\sum_{j=1}^{n} a_{ij} X_i = S_i \ (i = 1, 2, 3 \ldots\ldots m)$ are called slack variables.

"Slack variables are also defined as the non negative variables which are added in the LHS of the constraints to convert the inequality '≤' into an equation."

(2) If the constraints of a general LPP be

$$\sum_{j=1}^{n} a_{ij} X_i = b_i \ (i = 1, 2 \ldots\ldots m)$$

then non negative variables S_i which are introduced to convert the inequalities '≥' to

equalities $\sum_{j=1}^{n} a_{ij} X_i - S_i = b_i (i = 1, 2, 3 \ldots\ldots m)$ are called surplus variables.

"Surplus variables are defined as the non-negative variables which are removed from the LHS of the constraint to convert the inequality '≥' into an equation."

(3) If the constraints of a general LPP be

$$\sum_{j=1}^{n} a_{ij} X_i = b_i (i = 1, 2 \ldots\ldots m)$$

then the non-negative variables A_i are introduced to convert the equality into standard form of LPP.

$\sum_{j=1}^{n} a_{ij} X_i + A_i = b_i (i = 1, 2........m)$

Artificial variables are also defined as the non-negative variables which are added in the LHS of the constraints to convert equality into the stanard form of sumplex.

(4) If a variable is unrestricted in sign, then it can be expressed as a difference of two non-negative variable. i.e. X_1 is unrestricted in sign, then $X_1 = X_1' - X_1''$, where X_1', X_2'' are ≥ 0.

2.8 Solution of a LPP

In general, we use the following three methods for the solution of a LPP.

(i) Graphical Method

(ii) Simplex Method

(iii) Big-M Method

(iv) Two-Phase Method

2.9 Advantages of Linear programming Techniques

The main advantages of linear programming are given below:

1. It indicates how the available resources can be used in the best way.
2. It helps in attaining the optimum use of the productive resources and manpower.
3. It improves the quality of decisions.
4. It also reflects the drawbacks of the production process.
5. The necessary modifications of the mathematical solutions is also possible by using Linear programming.
7. It helps in re-evaluation of a basic plan with changing conditions.

2.10 Practice Problem

1. A manufacturer produces two types of model M_1 and M_2. Each model of the type M_1 requires 4 hrs of grinding and 2hrs of polishing; whereas each model of the type M_2 requires 2 hrs

of grinding and 5 hrs of polishing. The manufacturers have 2 grinders and 3 polishers. Each grinder works 40 hrs a week and each polisher works for 60 hrs a week.

Profit on M_1 model is Rs. 3 and on model M_2 is Rs 4. Whatever is produced in a week is sold in the market. How should the manufacturer allocate his production capacity to the two types of models, so that he may make the maximum profit in a week?

2. A person requires 10,12 and 12 units chemicals A, B and C respectively for his garden. A liquid product contains 5, 2 and 1 units of A , B, and C respectively per jar. A dry product contains 1, 2 and, 4 units of A, B, C per carton. If the liquid product sells for Rs. 3 per jar and the dry product sells for Rs 2 per carton, how many of each should be purchased, in order to minimize the total cost and meet the requirements.

3. A paper mill produces two grades of paper namely X and Y. Because of raw material restrictions, it cannot produce more than 400 ton of grade X and 300 tons of grades Y in a week. There are 160 production hrs in a week. It requires 0.2 and 0.4 hrs to produce a ton of products X and Y respectively with corresponding profits of Rs 200 and Rs 500 per ton. Formulate the above as a LPP to maximize profit and find the optimum product mix.

4. A company manufactures two products A and B. Each units of B takes twice as long to produce as one unit of A and if the company were to produce only A, it would have time to produce 2000 units per day. The availability of the raw materials is sufficient to produce 1500 units per day of both A and B combined. Product B requiring a special ingredient only 600 units can be made per day. If A fetches a profit of Rs. 2 per unit and B a profit of Rs. 4 per unit, find the optimum product mix by graphical method.

5. An animal food company must produce 200 kg of a mixture consisting of ingredients x_1 and x_2 daily. x_1 costs Rs. 3/- per kg. and x_2 costs Rs. 8/- per kg. No more than 80 kg. of x_1 can be used and at least 60 kg of x_2 must be used. Formulate a L.P.

model to minimize the cost.

6. A company produces two types of Hats. Each hat of the first type requires twice as much labour time as the second type. If all hats are of the second type only, the company can produce a total of 500 hats a day. The market limits daily sales of the first and second type to 150 and 250 hats. Assuming that the profits per hats are Rs 8 and Rs. 5 for hat A and B respectively. Formulate the problem as a linear programming model in order to determine the number of hats to be produce of each type so as to maximize the profits.

7. Egg contains 6 units of vitamin A per gram and 7 units of vitamin B per gram and cost 12 paise per gram. Milk contain 8 units of vitamin A per gram and 12 units of vitamin B per gram and cost 20 paise per gram. The daily minimum requirement of vitamin A and vitamin B are 100 units and 120 units respectively. Find the optimum product mix.

8.The standard weight of a special purpose brick is 5 kg and it contains two ingredients B_1 and B_2, B_1 cost Rs 5 per kg. and B_2 costs Rs. 8 per kg. Strength considerations dictate that the brick contains not more than 4 kg of B_1 and a minimum of 2 kg of B_2 since the demand for product is likely to be related to the price of the brick. Formulate the above problem as a L.P. model.

9. A company produces two types of leather belts A and B. A is of superior quality and B is of inferior quality. The respective profits are Rs. 10 and Rs.5 per belt. The supply of raw materials is sufficient for making 850 belts per day. For belt A, a special type of buckle is required and 500 are available per day. There are 700 buckles available for belt B per day. Belt A needs twice as much time as that required for belt B and the company can produce 500 belts if all of them were of the type A. Formulate a L.P. model for the above problem.

Objective Question:

1. Each constraints in an LP model is expressed as an
   (a) Inequality with ≥ sign

(b) Inequality with ≤ sign
(c) Equation with = sign
(d) Non of the above

2. A constraints in an LP model restricts
   (a) Value of the objective function
   (b) Value of a decision variable
   (c) Use of the available resources
   (d) All of the above

3. Constraints in an LP model represents
   (a) Limitations
   (b) Requirements
   (c) Balancing limitations and requirements
   (d) All of the above.

4. Linear programming is a
   (a) Constrained optimization technique
   (b) Technique for economic allocation of limited resources
   (c) Mathematical technique
   (d) All of the above

5. Non-negativity condition in an LP model implies
   (a) A positive coefficient of variables in objective function
   (b) A positive coefficient of variables in any constraint
   (c) Non-negative value of resources
   (d) None of the above

6. The best use of linear programming technique is to find an optimal use of
   (a) Money
   (b) Manpower
   (c) Machine
   (d) All of the above

7. Which of the following is not a characteristics of LP model
   (a) Alternative course of action
   (b) An objective function of maximization type
   (c) Limited amount of resources
   (d) Non-negativity condition on the value of decision variables

8. Maximization of objective function in LP model means
   (a) Value occurs at allowable set of decisions
   (b) Highest value is chosen among allowable decisions
   (c) Neither of above
   (d) Both (a) and (b)

9. Before formulating a formal LP model, it is better to
   (a) Express each constraints in words
   (b) Express the objective function in words
   (c) Decision variables are identified verbally
   (d) All of the above

10. Which of the following is not the characteristic of linear programming
    (a) Resources must be limited
    (b) Only one objective function
    (c) Parameters value remains constant during planning period
    (d) The problem must be of minimization type

Answer: 1(d), 2 (d), 3 (d), 4 (d), 5(d), 6(d), 7 (b), 8 (a), 9(d), 10.(d)

Chapter **3**

Graphical Method

Course outline

3.1 Introduction
3.2 Graphical method
3.3 Procedure of solving LPP by Graphical Method
3.4 Example
3.5 Cases
3.6 Practice Problem

3.1 Introduction:

After having formulated the LP problems as given in chapter 2, the linear programming problems can be solved by graphical methods.

3.2 Graphical Method:

If the objectives function Z is a function of two variables only then the problem can be solved by graphical method. A problem of three variables can be also solved by this method, but it is complicated enough.

3.3 Procedure of solving LPP by Graphical Method

Step 1. Formulates the problem into LP model.

Step 2. Consider each inequality constraints as equation.

Step 3. Plot each equation on the graph as each will geometrically represent a straight line.

Step 4. Shade the feasible region. Every point on the line will satisfy the equation of line. If the inequality constraints corresponding to that line is '≤' then the region below the line lying in the first quadrant (due to non-negativity of variables) is shaded. For the inequality constraints with '≥' sign, the region above the line in the first quadrant is shaded.

The point lying in common region will satisfy all the constraints simultaneously. Thus the common region obtained it is called the feasible region.

Step 5. Choose the convenient value of Z (say = 0) and plot the objective function line.

Step 6. Stretch the objective function line till the extreme points of the feasible region. In the maximization case, this line will stop farthest from the origin and passing through at least one corner of the feasible region. In the minimization case, this line will stop nearest to the origin and passing through at least one corner of the feasible region.

Step 7. Find the coordinates of the extreme points selected in **Step 6.** and find the maximum or minimum value of Z.

3.4 Examples:

Example 1. Find a geometrical interpretation and solution as well for the following LP problem:

Maximize (z) = $3 X_1 + 5 X_2$

Subject to constraints

$X_1 + 2 X_2 \leq 2000$

$X_1 + X_2 \leq 1500$

$X_2 \leq 600$

And $X_1, X_2 \leq 0$

Solution: Replace all the inequalities of the constraints by equation

$X_1 + 2 X_2 = 2000$ If $X_1 = 0$ then $X_2 = 1000$; $X_2 = 0$ then $X_1 = 2000$.

$X_1 + X_2 = 1500$ If $X_1 = 0$ then $X_2 = 1500$; $X_2 = 0$ then $X_1 = 1500$

$X_2 = 600$ this implies that $X_1 = 0$

Therefore $X_1 + 2 X_2 = 2000$ passes through (0, 1000) (2000,0)

$X_1 + X_2 = 1500$ passes through (1500, 0) (0, 1500)

$X_2 = 600$ passes through (0, 600)

Plot each equation on the graph.

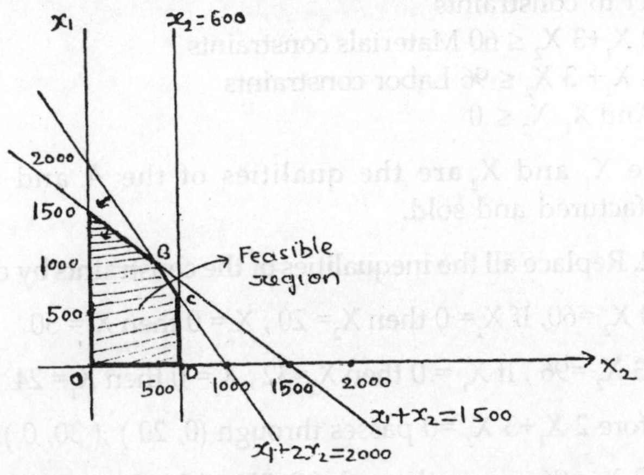

The feasible region is ABCD.

B and C are the point of intersection of lines $X_1+2X_2=2000$, $X_1+X_2=1500$ and $X_1+2X_2=2000$, $X_2=600$ on solving we get B= (1000, 500) C = (800, 600)

Now

Corner points	Value of $Z=3X_1+5X_2$
A (1500,0)	4500
B (1000, 500)	5500 (Maximum Value)
C (800,600)	5400
D (0,600)	3000

Therefore, the Maximum value of Z occurs at B (1000 ,500) ; hence the optimal solution is $X_1=1000$,and $X_2=500$.

Example 2. A and B are two product to be manufactured unit profits are Rs 40 and Rs 35 respectively. Maximum materials available are 60 kgs and labour 96 hrs. Each units of A needs 2 kg of materials and 3 man-hours, whereas each units of B needs 4 Kg of materials and 3 man-hours. Find optimal level of A and B to be manufactured.

Solution:

Step 1. Maximize (z) = $40X_1+35X_2$

Subject to constraints

$2X_1+3X_2 \leq 60$ Materials constraints

$4X_1+3X_2 \leq 96$ Labor constraints

And $X_1, X_2 \leq 0$

Where X_1 and X_2 are the qualities of the A and B to be manufactured and sold.

Step 2. Replace all the inequalities of the constraints by equation

$2X_1+3X_2 = 60$, If $X_1 = 0$ then $X_2 = 20$; $X_2 = 0$ then $X_1 = 30$

$4X_1+3X_2 = 96$, If $X_1 = 0$ then $X_2 = 32$; $X_2 = 0$ then $X_1 = 24$

Therefore $2X_1+3X_2 = 0$ passes through (0, 20) ,(30, 0).

$4X_1+3X_2 = 96$ passes through (0, 32) , (24, 0).

Plot each equation on the graph.

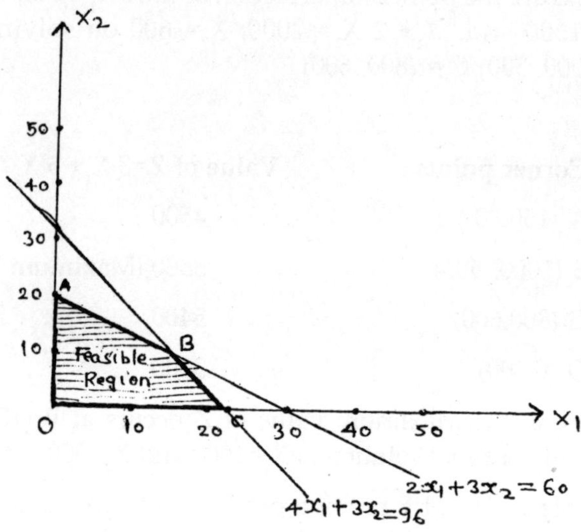

The feasible region is ABC.

B is the point of intersection of lines $2X_1+3X_2 = 60$ and $4X_1+3X_2 = 96$ on solving we get B = (18 , 8)

Corner points	Value of $Z= 40X_1+35X_2$
A (0, 20)	700

B (18, 8) 1000 (Maximum value)

C (24, 0) 960

Therefore, the maximum value of Z occurs at B (18, 8) . Hence the optimal solution is X_1=18, X_2= 8.

Example3. Solve the following LPP by Graphical method.

Minimize (Z) = $20 X_1 + 10 X_2$

Subject to $X_1 + 2 X_2 \leq 40$

$3 X_1 + X_2 \geq 30$

$4 X_1 + 3X_2 \geq 60$

And $X_1, X_2 \geq 0$

Solution: Convert all the inequalities of the constraints by equation

$X_1 + 2 X_2 = 40$ If X_1=0 then X_2= 20 ; X_2= 0 then X_1=40.

$3 X_1 + X_2 = 30$ If X_1=0 then X_2=30 ; X_2=0 then X_1=10.

$4 X_1 + 3X_2 = 60$ If X_1=0 then X_2=20; X_2=0 then X_1= 15.

Therefore $X_1 + 2 X_2 = 40$ passes through (40, 20).

$3 X_1 + X_2 = 30$ passes through (10, 30).

$4 X_1 + 3X_2 = 60$ passes through (15, 20).

Plot each equation on the graph.

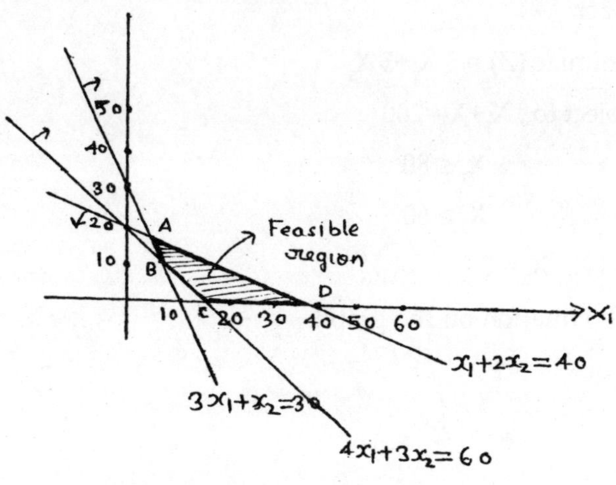

The feasible region is ABCD.

A, B and C are the point of intersection of lines $X_1+2X_2=40$, $3X_1+X_2=30$ and

$3X_1+X_2=30$, $4X_1+3X_2=60$ on solving we get A = (4, 18) , B = (6, 12).

Corner points	Value of Z= $20X_1+10X_2$
A (4, 18)	260
B (6, 12)	240 (Minimum value)
C (15, 0)	300
D (40, 0)	400

Therefore the minimum value of Z occurs at B (6 , 12). Hence the optimal solution is $X_1 = 6$, $X_2 = 12$.

Example 4.

An animal feed company must produce 200kg of a mixture consisting of ingredients X_1 and X2. The ingredient X_1 Costs Rs 3 per kg and X_2 cost Rs 5 per kg. No more than 80 kg of X_1 can be used and at least 60 kg of X_2 must be used. Find the minimum cost mixture.

Solution: The mathematical formulation of given linear problem is as under

Minimize (Z) = $3X_1+5X_2$

Subject to , $X_1+X_2=200$

$X_1 \leq 80$

$X_2 \geq 60$

And $X_1, X_2 = 0$

Plot each equation on the graph.

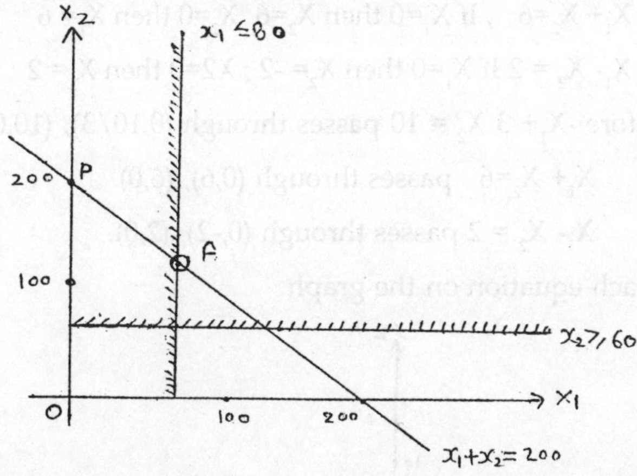

It can be seen that there is no feasible region in this case due to the constraints but there is only a feasible point (A), whose co-ordinates are

$X_1 = 80$, $X_2 = 120$

Minimum cost (z) = 3 × 80 + 5 × 120

= Rs 840

Hence, the optimal mix of the animal feed is 80 kg of product X_1, 120 kg of produce X_2 at minimum cost = Rs 840.

Example 5. Solve the following LP problem by graphical method.

Minimize (z) = $- X_1 + 2 X_2$

Subject to

$-X_1 + 3 X_2 \leq 10$

$X_1 + X_2 \leq 6$

$X_1 - X_2 \leq 2$

$X_1, X_2 \geq 0$

Solution: Convert all the inequalities of the constraints by equation

$-X_1 + 3 X_2 = 10$, If $X_1 = 0$ then $X_2 = 10/3$; $X_2 = 0$ then $X_1 = -10$.

$X_1 + X_2 = 6$, If $X_1=0$ then $X_2=6$; $X_2=0$ then $X_1= 6$

$X_1 - X_2 = 2$ If $X_1=0$ then $X_2= -2$; X2=0 then $X_1= 2$

Therefore $-X_1+ 3 X_2 = 10$ passes through (0,10/3), (10,0).

$X_1+ X_2=6$ passes through (0,6), (6,0).

$X_1- X_2 = 2$ passes through (0,-2), (2,0).

Plot each equation on the graph.

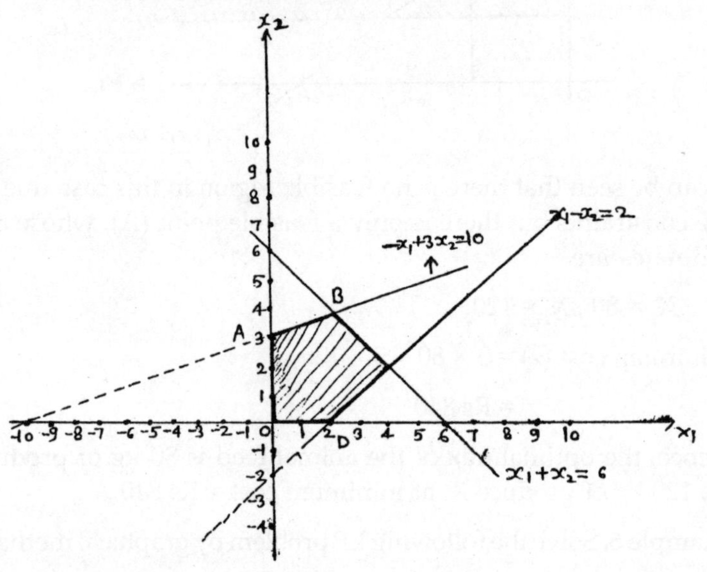

The feasible region OABCD.

B and C are the point of intersection of lines $-X_1+ 3 X_2 = 10$, $X_1+ X_2=6$ and $X_1- X_2 = 2$, $X_1+ X_2=6$ on solving we get B= (2,4) C= (4,2).

Corner points	**Value of Z= $- X_1+ 2 X_2$**	
A (0,3)	6	
B (2,4)	6	
C (4,2)	0	
D (2,0)	-2	**(Minimum Value**

)

Therefore the minimum value Z occurs at D (2,0). Hence the optimal solution is $X_1=2$, $X_2=0$ and Min (Z)= -2.

3.5 Cases:

(1) Multiple optimal solution:

Example: Solve the LPP by graphical method

Maximize (Z) = 100 X + 40 X

Subject to

$5X_1 + 2X_2 \le 1000$

$3X_1 + 2X_2 \le 900$

$X_1 + 2X_2 \le 500$

And $X_1, X_2 \le 0$

Solution: Convert all the inequalities of the constraints by equation

$5X_1 + 2X_2 = 1000$ If $X_1=0$ then $X_2=500$; $X_2=0$ then $X_1=200$.

$3X_1 + 2X_2 = 900$ If $X_1=0$ then $X_2= 450$; $X_2=0$ then $X_1=300$.

$X_1 + 2X_2 = 500$ If $X_1=0$ then $X_2= 250$; $X_2=0$ then $X_1=500$

Therefore, $5X_1 + 2X_2 = 1000$, passes through (0,500) , (200,0).

$3X_1 + 2X_2 = 900$ passes through (0,450), (300,0).

$X_1 + 2X_2 = 500$ passes through (0, 500), (250,0).

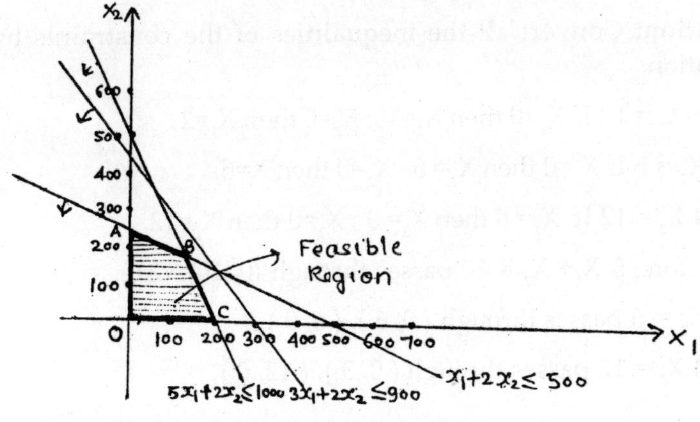

Plot each equation on the graph.

The feasible region is given by OABC.

B is the point of intersection of lines $X_1 + 2X_2 = 500$, $5X_1 + 2X_2 = 1000$ on solving it we get B (125, 187.5).

Corner points	Value of $Z = 100X_1 + 40X_2$
A (0, 250)	10,000
B (125, 187.5)	20,000 (Maximum value of Z)
C (200,0)	20,000 (Maximum value of Z)

Therefore, the maximum value of Z occurs at two vertices B & b C gives the maximum value of Z.

Thus, there are multiple optimum solutions for the LPP.

(2) Unbounded Solutions:

Example: Use graphical method to solve the LPP

$\text{Max}(Z) = 3X_1 + 2X_2$

Subject to

$5X_1 + X_2 \geq 10$

$X_1 + X_2 \geq 6$

$X_1 + 4X_2 \geq 12$

And $X_1, X_2 \geq 0$

Solution: Convert all the inequalities of the constraints by equation.

$5X_1 + X_2 = 10$ If $X_1=0$ then $X_2=10$; $X_2=0$ then $X_1=2$.

$X_1 + X_2 = 6$ If $X_1=0$ then $X_2=6$; $X_2=0$ then $X=6$.

$X_1 + 4X_2 = 12$ If $X_1=0$ then $X_2=3$; $X_2=0$ then $X_1=12$.

Therefore, $5X_1 + X_2 = 10$ passes through (0, 10), (2,0).

$X_1 + X_2 = 6$ passes through (0, 6), (6, 0).

$X_1 + 4X_2 = 12$ passes through (0, 3), (12, 0).

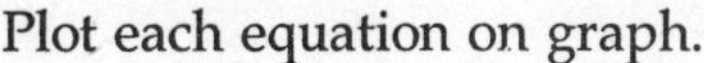

Plot each equation on graph.

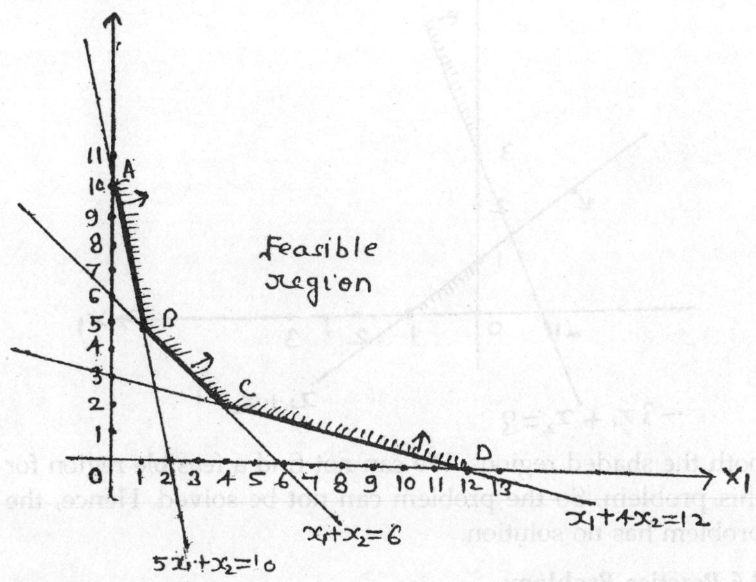

The feasible region is unbounded. Thus, the Maximum value of Z occurs at infinity. Hence, the problem has an unbounded solution.

(3) No feasible Solution:

When there is no feasible region formed by the constraints then the problem has no feasible solution.

Example. Solve the following LPP.

Max (Z) = $X_1 + X_2$

Subject to $X_1 + X_2 \leq 1$

$-3X_1 + X_2 \leq 3$

$X_1, X_2 \leq 0$

Solution:

After plotting the graph we get

In the above graph, there being no point (X_1, X_2) common to

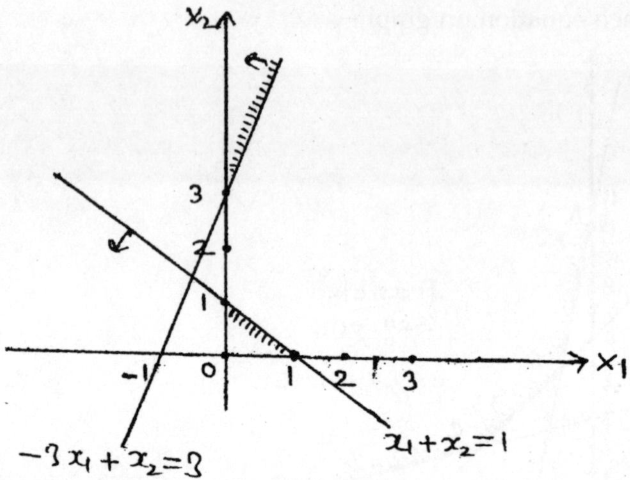

both the shaded regions. We can not find a feasible region for this problem. So the problem can not be solved. Hence, the problem has no solution.

3.6 Practice Problem:

Objective Question:

1. The graphical model of LP problem uses
   (a) Objective function equation
   (b) Constraints
   (c) Linear equations
   (d) All of the above
2. A feasible solution to a LP problem
   (a) Must satisfy all of the problem's constraints simultaneously
   (b) Need not satisfy all of the constraints only some of them
   (c) Must be corner point of the feasible region
   (d) Must optimize the value of the objective function.
3. An Iso- profit line represents
   (a) An infinite number of solution all of which yield the same cost.
   (b) An infinite number of solutions all of which yield the same profit.
   (c) An infinite number of optimal solutions

(d) A boundary of the feasible region.

4. A constraints in an LP model becomes redundant because
   (a) Two iso-profit line may be parallel to each other.
   (b) The solution is unbounded.
   (c) This constraint is not satisfied by the solution values.
   (d) None of the above.
5. If two constraints do not intersects in the positive quadrant of the graph, then
   (a) The problem is infeasible
   (b) The solution is unbounded.
   (c) One of the constraints is redundant.
   (d) None of the above.
6. Constraints in LP problem are called active if they
   (a) Represent optimal solution.
   (b) At optimality do not consume all the available resources.
   (c) Both of (a) and (b).
   (d) None of the above
7. The solution space (region) of an LP problem is unbounded due to
   (a) An incorrect formulation of the LP model.
   (b) Objective function is unbounded
   (c) Neither (a) nor (b)
   (d) Both (a) and (b)
8. Alternative solutions exist of an LP model when
   (a) One of the constraints is redundant.
   (b) Objective function equation is parallel to one of the constraints.
   (c) Two constraints are parallel.
   (d) All of the above.
9. While solving a LP problem infeasibility may be removed by
   (a) Adding another a constraints.
   (b) Adding another variable.
   (c) Removing a constraints.
   (d) Removing a variable.

10. If a iso-profit line yielding the optimal solution coincides with a constraints line , then
    (a) The solution is unbounded.
    (b) The solution is infeasible
    (c) The constraints which coincides is redundant.
    (d) None of the above.

Answer: 1 (d), 2 (a), 3 (b), 4 (d), 5 (a), 6 (a), 7 (c), 8 (b), 9 (c), 10 (d)

Problems:

1. Solve the following LP problems:

(i) Max (Z) $= 4X_1 + 4X_2$

Subject to $X_1 + 2X_2 \le 10$

$6X_1 + 6X_2 \le 36$

$X_1 \le 6$

And $X_1, X_2 \ge 0$

(ii) Max (Z) $= 4X_1 + 2X_2$

Subject to $-X_1 + 2X_2 \le 6$

$-X_2 + X_2 \le 2$

And $X_1, X_2 \ge 0$

(iii) Min(Z) $= 4X_1 - 2X_2$

Subject to $X_1 + X_2 \le 14$

$3X_1 + 2X_2 \ge 36$

$2X_1 + X_2 \le 24$

And $X_1, X_2 \ge 0$

(iv) Min (Z) $= 20X_1 + 10X_2$

Subject to $X_1 + 2X_2 \le 40$

$3X_1 + X_2 \ge 30$

$4X_1 + 3X_2 \ge 60$

And $X_1, X_2 \ge 0$

2. A furniture manufacturer makes two products : Chairs and tables. Processing of these products is done on two machines A and B. A chair requires 2 hrs on machine A and 6 hrs on machine B. A table requires 5 hrs on machine A and no time on machine B. There are 16 hrs per day available on machine A and 30 hrs on machine B. Profit gained by manufacturer from a chair and a table is Rs 2 and Rs10, respectively. Solve this problem to find the daily production of each of the two products.

Ans. X_1 and X_2 = **Number** of chairs and tables produced, respectively.

$$\text{Max}(Z) = 2X_1 + 10X_2$$

Subject to

$$2X_1 + 5X_2 \le 16$$

$$6X_1 \le 30$$

And $X_1, X_2 \ge 0$

And $X_1 = 0$, $X_2 = 3.2$ and Max (Z) = Rs 32

3. An aviation fuel manufacturer sells two types of fuel **A** and **B**. Type**A** fuel is 25% grade **1** gasoline, 25% of grade **2** gasoline and 50% of grade **3** gasoline. Type **B** fuel is 50% of grade **2** gasoline and 50% of grade **3** gasoline. Available for production are 500 liters per hour grade **1** and 200 liters per hour of grade **2** and grade **3** each. Costs are 60 paise per liter for grade **1**, 120 paise for grade **2** and 100 paise for grade **3** . Type **A** can be sold at Rs. 7.5 per liter and **B** can be sold at Rs 9 per liter.

4. A company manufactures two products X_1 and X_2 on three machines A, B and C. X_1 requires 1 hrs on machine A and 1 hrs on machine B and yields a revenue of Rs 3/- . Product X_2 requires 2 hrs on machine A and 1 hrs on machine B and 1 hrs on machine C and yields revenue of Rs. 5/-. In the coming planning period the available time of three machines A, B and C are 2000 hrs, 1500 hrs and 600 hrs respectively. Find the optimal product mix.

Chapter 4

Simplex Method

Course outline

- 4.1 Introduction
- 4.2 Simplex method
- 4.3 Big – M method
- 4.4 Duality in LPP
- 4.5 Two phase method
- 4.6 Degeneracy in Simplex method
- 4.7 Practice Problem

4.1 Introduction

The two variable problems of the LPP can be solved by the graphical method, but it is very complicated to solve the three or more variable problem by using the graphical method. In such cases, a simplex and most widely used simplex method is adopted, which was developed by G. Dantzig in 1947.

The simplex method provides an algorithm which is based on the fundamental theorem of linear programming.

4.2 Simplex Method

The simplex algorithm is an iteractive (step-by -step) procedure for solving LP problems. It consist of –

Step. 1 Express the problem in standard form.

Step. 2 Find the initial basic feasible solution.

Step. 3 Perform optimality test.

Step. 4 Iterate towards an optimal solution.

Step.1 Express the problem in standard form:

(i) check whether the objective function of the given LPP is to be maximized or minimized then we have to convert it

$$\text{Min } (z) = \text{Max } (-Z)$$

(ii) Check whether all b_i (i=1,2,3......m) are positive. If any one of b_i is negative then multiply the inequation of the constraints by (-1) so as to get all b_i to be positive.

(iii) After that express the problem in standard form by introducing slack, surplus variables, to convert the inequation into equations.

Problem:

$$\text{Max } (Z) = C_1 X_1 + C_2 X_2 + \text{............} C_n X_n + 0.\ S_2 + \text{.......} + 0.\ S_m$$

Subject to

$$a_{11} X_1 + a_{12} X_2 + \text{..........}\ a_{1n} X_n \leq B_1$$

$$a_{21} X_1 + a_{22} X_2 + \text{.........} + a_{21} X_n \leq B_2$$

|

|

|

$$a_{mi} X_1 + a_{m2} X_2 + \text{............} + a_{mn} X_n \leq B_m$$

$$X_1, X_2, \text{...........} X_n \geq 0$$

Standard form of Simplex

$$\text{Max } (Z) = C_1 X_1 + C_2 X_2 + \text{.........} C_n X_n + 0.S_1 + 0.S_2 + \text{.........} + 0.S_m$$

Subject to

$$a_{11} X_1 + a_{12} X_2 + \text{.........}\ a_{1n} X_n + S_1 = B_1$$

$$a_{21} X_1 + a_{22} X_2 + \text{.........} + a_{21} X_n + S_2 = B_2$$

|

|

|

$$a_{mi} X_1 + a_{m2} X_2 + \text{............} + a_{mn} X_n + S_m = B_m$$

$$X_1, X_2, \text{............} X_n \geq 0$$

Step.2 Find the initial basic feasible solution:

(i) In the simplex method, a start is made with a feasible solution, which we shall get by assuming that the profit earned is zero. This will be so when decision variables X_1, X_2, X_3 ....and X_n each equal to zero. These variables are called non -basic variables.

(ii) Substituting $X_1 = X_2 = X_3 = ... = X_n = 0$ in equation (2) we get $s_1 = b_1$, $s_2 = b_2$ ....$s_m = b_m$ which is called initial basic feasible solution. Note that Z=0 for this solution.

(iii) Variables s_1, s_2 ....s_m are called **basic variables.**

(iv) The problem in standard form and the solution obtained above are now expressed in the form of a table, called the simplex table.

			C_j C_1 C_2 C_3..........C_n 0 0 0 0	
C_B	B_m	X_B	X_1 X_2 X_3..........X_n S_1 S_2 S_3...............S_n	Min ratio
Cs_1 Cs_2 ⋮ Cs_m	S_1 S_2 ⋮ S_m	B1 B2 ⋮ B_m	a_{11} a_{12} a_{13}...a_{1n} 1 0 0 ....0 a_{21} a_{22} a_{23}...a_{2n} 0 1 0............0 ⋮ a_{m1} a_{m2} a_{m3}...a_{mn} 0 0 0 1	
Z= ? $Cs_m.B_m$		Z_j= ? $Cs_m.Xj$	0 0 0......0 0 0 0 0	
--	--	Cj-Zj	C_1- Z_j, C_2- Z_2..... C_n-Z_n 0 0 0 0	

C_j : Objective row (Coefficient of variable in objective function) It remain unchanged during succeeding table.

C_b : Objective column (Coefficient of current basic variable in objective function)

B_m: Basic variables in basic. Initially basic variable are slack variables.

X_B: Values of basic variables column when $X_1 = X_2 = X_3 = \ldots\ldots\ldots X_n = 0$

Body Matrix: Coefficient of decision (Non-basic) variables in constraints set (a_{ij})

Identity Matrix: Coefficient of slack variables in the initial table.

Z: It represents profit or loss [$Z = \Sigma\ (s_m \times B_m)$]

$C_j - Z_j$: It presents index row

Step 3. perform optimality test:

Calculate the elements of index row (C_j-Z_j) ; if all the elements in index row are negative, then current solution is optimum basic feasible solution if not then go for next step.

Step 4. Iterate towards an optimal solution.

(a) Revision of current simplex table

(1) Identify key column, with largest positive number in the index row. Non-basic variable at the top of this column is entering variable for the next iteration.

(2) Identify key row, corresponding to smallest non-negative ratio found by dividing the values.

(3) Identify key element, the non-zero positive element at the intersection of key column and key row. Encircle the key element.

(b) Construct new simplex table.

(1) Calculate the new values for the key row by dividing every element of key row by key number.

(2) Entries in variable and objective column of key row are taken respective from column value of variable and objective row.

(3) The new values of the elements in the remaining rows (other than those in objective and variable column which remain the same as in previous table) are calculated by using following formula.

(4) Go to step 3 and repeat the procedure until either an optimal solution is reached or there is an indication of unbounded solution.

Example: 1 Solve the following LPP by using Simplex method

Max (z) = $6X_1 + 4X_2$

Subject to $X_1 + 2X_2 \leq 720$

$2X_1 + X_2 = 780$

$$\text{New No.} = \text{Old No.} - \frac{(\text{Associated no. in key row}) \times (\text{Corresponding no. in key column})}{\text{Key element}}$$

$X_1 = 320$

Solution:

Step. 1 Convert the following LPP into standard form.

Max (z) = $6X_1 + 4X_2 + 0.S_1 + 0.S_2 + 0.S_3$

Subject to $X_1 + 2X_2 + S_1 = 720$

$2X_1 + X_2 + S_2 \leq 780$

$X_1 + S_3 \leq 320$

$X_1, X_2 = 0$

Step. 2 Initial basic feasible solution

$X_1 = 0$ and $X_2 = 0$ in the above equation then we have $S_1 = 720$, $S_2 = 780$ and $S_3 = 320$

1st table

		Cj	6	4	0	0	0	
C_B	B	X_B	X1	X2	S1	S2	S3	Min Ratio
0	S1	720	1	2	1	0	0	720
0	S2	780	2	1	0	1	0	390
0	S3	320	(1)	0	0	0	1	320 ← Key row
Z=0		Zj=	0	0	0	0	0	
		Cj-Zj	↑6	4	0	0	0	

Key column

2nd table

C_B	B	X_B	Cj: 6 X_1	4 X_2	0 S_1	0 S_2	0 S_3	Min Ratio
0	S_1	120	0	0	1	-2	(3)	40 ← Key row
4	X_2	140	0	1	0	1	-2	--
6	X_1	320	1	0	0	0	1	320
Z=2480		Z_j=	6	4	0	4	-2	
		C_j-Z_j	0	0	0	-4	2	

↑ Key column

3rd table

C_B	B	X_B	Cj: 6 X_1	4 X_2	0 S_1	0 S_2	0 S_3	Min Ratio
0	S_3	40	0	0	1/3	-2/3	1	
4	X_2	220	0	1	2/3	-1/3	0	
6	X_1	280	1	0	-1/3	2/3	0	
Z=2560		Z_j=	6	4	2/3	8/3	0	
		C_j-Z_j	0	0	-2/3	-8/3	2	

Since Cj - Zj ≤ 0 therefore we have

Optimal Solution: Z= 2560

X1=280, X2 = 220

Example 2: Use simplex method to solve the L.P.P

Max (z) = $3X_1 + 2X_2$

subject to

$X_1 + X_2 \leq 4$

$X_1 - X_2 \leq 2$

$X_1, X_2 \geq 0$

Solution:

Step.1 Convert the above problem into standard form of LPP.

Max (Z) = $3X_1 + 2X_2 + 0.S_1 + 0.S_2$

Subject to

$$X_1 + X_2 + S_1 = 4$$

$$X_1 - X_2 + S_2 = 2$$

Step.2 Initial basic feasible solution

Put $X_1 = X_2 = 0$ in the above equation then we have $S_1=4$ and $S_2=2$

1st table

		Cj	6	4	0	0		
C_B	B	X_B	X1	X2	S1	S2	Min Ratio	
0	S1	4	1	1	1	0	4/1=4	
0	S2	2	(1)	-1	0	1	2/1=2	← Key row
Z=0		Zj=	0	0	0	0		
		Cj-Zj	↑3	2	0	0		

Key column

2nd table

		Cj	6	4	0	0		
C_B	B	X_B	X_1	X_2	S_1	S_2	Min Ratio	
0	S_1	2	0	(2)	1	-1	2/1=4	← Key row
3	X_1	2	1	-1	0	1	--	
Z=6		Zj=	3	-3	0	0		
		Cj-Zj	0	5↑	0	0		

Key column

3rd table

		Cj	6	4	0	0	
C_B	B	X_B	X_1	X_2	S_1	S_2	Min Ratio
2	S_1	1	0	1	1/2	-1/2	--
3	X_1	3	1	0	1/2	1/2	--
Z=6		Zj=	3	2	5/2	1/2	
		Cj-Zj	0	0	-5/2	-1/2	

Since all Cj - Zj ≤ 0, therefore the solution is optimum. The optimal solution is Maximum (z) =11 $X_1 = 3$ and $X_2 = 1$.

4.3 Big - M Method

If at least one constriants of the LPP are in '≥' or '=' then this type of problem can be solved by using Big-M method (artificial variable techniques). In these problem we cannot get the starting basic matrix B = Im. So to avoid this difficulty we add one more variable to each of such constraints. These variables are called **'artificial variables'.**

Procedure of the Big-M method:

There are the following steps involved in the Big-M method for solving the LPP.

Step.1 Express the problem in to the standard form o the LPP.

Step.2 Change the inequalities (≥ and =) by the following rule.

For example.

(i) $a_1 X_1 + a_2 X_2 + \ldots\ldots + a_n X_n \geq b_1$ can be changed by adding surplus variable with negative sign and non-nbegative artificial variable.

(i) $a_1 X_1 + a_2 X_2 + \ldots\ldots + a_n X_n - S_1 + A_1 = b_1$

(ii) $a_1 X_1 + a_2 X_2 + \ldots\ldots + a_n X_n = b_1$ can be changed by adding non-negative artificial variable

Step.3 Now change the objective function by multiplying the large penalty (-M for maximization and M for minimization) with the artificial variable and add it to the objective function. (In the objective function of the Big-M method we can add only the slack and artificial variables, we can't use surplus variables).

Step.4 Construct the table and solve the modified LPP by simplex method, until any one of the three cases may arise.

1. If no artificial variable appears in the basis and the optimality conditions are satisfied, then the current solution is an optimal basic feasible solution.
2. If at least one artificial variable in the basis with zero values and the optimality condition is satisfied, then the current solution is an optimal basic feasible solution. (Though degenerated solution).

3. If at least one artificial variable appears in the basis at positive values and the optimality condition is satisfied, then the original problem has no feasible solution. The solution satisfies the constraints but does not optimize the objective function, since it contains a very large penalty M and it is called the pseudo optimal solution.
4. While applying simplex method, whenever an artificial variable happens to leave basis, we drop that artificial variable and remove all the entries corresponding to its column from the simplex table.

Example 1: Max (z) = $4X_1 + 5X_2 - 3X_3$

Subject to

$X_1 + X_2 + X_3 = 10$

$X_1 - X_2 \geq 1, 2x_1 + 3x_2 + x_3 \leq 30$

Solution :

Step.1 Convert the above problem into standard form of LPP.

Max (z) = $4X_1 + 5X_2 - 3X_3 + 0.S_1 + 0.S_2 - MA_1 - MA_2$

Subject to

$X_1 + X_2 + X_3 + A_1 = 10$

$X_1 - X_2 - S_1 + A_2 = 1$

$2X_1 + 3X_2 + X_3 + S_2 = 30$

Step. 2 Initial basic feasible solution

$X_1, X_2, X_3 = 0$ in the above equation then we have $A_1 = 10$, A= 1 and $S_2 = 30$

1st table

		Cj	4	5	-3	0	0	-M	-M	
CB	B	XB	X1	X2	X3	S1	S2	A1	A2	
-M	A1	10	1	1	1	0	0	1	0	10
-M	A2	1	(1)	-1	0	-1	0	0	1	1 ← Key row
0	S2	30	2	3	1	0	1	0	0	15
Z= -11M		Zj	-2M	0	-M	M	0	-M	-M	
		Cj-Zj	4+2M	5	-3+M	-M	0	0	0	

Key column

Entering Variable = X1
Leaving Variable = A2
2nd table

		Cj	4	5	-3	0	0	-M	
CB	B	XB	X1	X2	X3	S1	S2	A1	
-M	A1	9	0	2	1	1	0	1	9/2=4.5 ← Key ro
4	X1	1	1	-1	0	-1	0	0	--
0	S2	28	0	5	1	2	1	0	28/5=5.4
Z= -9M+4		Zj	4	(-2M-4)	-M	-M-4	0	-M	
		Cj-Zj	0	9+2M	-3+M	M+4	0	0	

↑ Key column

Entering Variable = X_2

Leaving Variable= A_1

3rd table

		Cj	4	5	-3	0	0	
CB	B	XB	X_1	X_2	X_3	S_1	S_2	
5	X_2	4.5	0	1	1/2	1/2	0	
4	X_1	5.5	1	0	1/2	-1/2	0	
0	S_2	50.5	0	6	3/2	5/2	1	
Z= 44.5		Zj	4	5	9/2	1/2	0	
		Cj-Zj	0	0	-15/2	-1/2	0	

Since all Cj- Zj ≤ 0 therefore, the solution is optimum. Thus, we get $X_1 = 5.5$

X_2=4.5 and Maximum (z)= 44.5

Example. 2 Solve the following LPP by using Big –M method

Min (z) = 600 X_1 + 500 X_2

Subject to

$2X_1 + X_2 \geq 80$

$X_1 + 2X_2 \geq 60$

$X_1, X_2 = 0$

Solution.

Step 1. Convert the above problem into standard form of the LP problem by using surplus and artificial variable.

Min (z)= $600X_1 + 500X_2 + 0.S_1 + 0.S_2 + M.A_1 + M.A_2$

Subject to

$2X_1 + X_2 - S_1 + A_1 = 80$

$X_1 + 2X_2 - S_2 + A_2 = 60$

And $X_1, X_2, S_1, S_2, A_1, A_2 \geq 0$

Step. 2 THe initial basic feasible solution.

X1 = X2 = S1 = S2 = 0

A1 = 80, A2 = 60

1st table

		Cj	600	500	0	0	M	M	
Cb	bi	Xb	X1	X2	S1	S2	A1	A2	
M	A1	80	2	1	-1	0	1	0	80/1=80
M	A2	60	1	(2)	0	-1	0	1	60/2= 30 ←
Z= 140 M		Zj = Cj- Zj =	3M 600- 3M	3M 500- 3M	-M M	-M M	-M 0	-M 0	
M	A1	50	(3/2)	0	-1	1/2	1	-	
500	X2	30	1/2	1	0	-1/2	0	-	
Z=150 0+50 M		Zj = CJ- Zj=	3M/2 +350- ↑	500 0	-M M	M/2 250-	250 M/2	- -	

		Cj	600	500	0	0			
M	A1	50	1	0	-2/3	1/3	-	-	
500	X2	50	0	1	1-3	2/3	-	-	
Z=8000 0/3		Zj = Cj Zj=	600 0	500 0	-700/3 700/3	-400/3 400/3	- -	- -	

Since all the numbers in the C_j - Z_j row are either zero or positive and also both artificial variables have been reduced to zero, an optimum solution has been arrived at with X_1 = 100/3 and X_2 = 40/3, at a total minimum cost (Z) = Rs. 80,000/3

4.4 Duality in linear Programming Problem:

Whenever the linear programming problem contains a large number of constraints and a smaller number of variables then the labour of computation can be considerably reduced by converting it into the dual and then solve it. Every LPP is associated with another linear programming problem called the dual of the problem. The original problem is called the 'Primal'.

Definition of the dual problem:

Let the primal problem be

Max (z)= $C_1X_1 + C_2X_2 + \ldots\ldots + C_n X_n$

subject to

$a_{11}X_1 + a_{12} X_2 + \ldots\ldots + a_{1n} X_n \leq b_1$

$a_{21}X_1 + a_{22} X_2 + \ldots\ldots + a_{2n} Xn \leq b_2$

$a_{m1}X_1 + a_{m2}X_2 + \ldots\ldots + a_{mn} X_n \leq b_m$

$X_1 , X_2, \ldots\ldots X_n \geq 0$

The dual of the problem is defined as

Min $(Z_d) = b_1 w_1 + b_2 w_2 + \ldots\ldots b_m w_m$

Subject to

$a_{11}w_1 + a_{21} w_2 + \ldots\ldots + a_{m1} w_n \geq c_1$

$a_{12}X_1 + a_{22}\, w_2 + \dots\dots\dots + a_{m2}\, w_n \geq c_2$

$a_{1n}X_1 + a_{2n}\, w_2 + \dots\dots\dots + a_{mn}\, w_n \geq c_m$

$w_1\ ,\ w_2, \dots\dots\dots\dots w_m \geq 0$

where w_1 , w_2 , $w_3 \dots\dots\dots w_m$ are called dual variable.

In matrix notation the primal and dual problems can be written as follows.

Primal :

Max (Zp) = CX

s.t. $Ax \leq b$

and $x \geq 0$

$$\text{where } x = \begin{pmatrix} X_1 \\ X_2 \\ : \\ : \\ X_n \end{pmatrix}$$

Dual :

Min (Zd) = $b'\, w$

s.t $A'\, w \geq c'$

and $w \geq 0$

$$\text{where } x = \begin{pmatrix} W_1 \\ W_2 \\ : \\ : \\ W_n \end{pmatrix}$$

Standard form of the primal

(a) All the constraints involve the sign $\leq$ if it is a problem of maximization.

(b) All the constraints involve the sign $\geq$ if it is a problem of minimization.

Formulation of Dual :

(1) Change the objective function of maximization in the primal into minimization in the dual and vice-versa.

(2) The number of variable in the primal will be the number of constraints in the dual and vice-versa.

(3) The cost of coefficients c_1 , c_2 , ...c_n in the objective function of the primal will be the RHS constant of the constraints in the dual and vice-versa.

(4) For the constraints of dual, transpose the body matrix of the primal problem.

(5) The variables in both the problems are non negative.

(6) If the variable in the primal is unrestricted in sign, then the corresponding constraints in the dual will be an equation and vice-versa.

Example 1: Write the dual of the following LPP.

$$\text{Max } (Z) = 3X_1 + X_2 + X_3$$

$$\text{Subject to } 4X_1 - X_2 \leq 8$$

$$8X_1 + X_2 + 3X_3 \geq 12$$

$$5X_1 - 6X_3 \leq 13, X_1, X_2, X_3 \geq 0$$

Solution : Express the problem into the standard form of the primal.

$$\text{Max } (Z) = 3X_1 + X_2 + X_3$$

Subject to

$$4X_1 - X_2 + 0.X_3 \leq 8$$

$$-8X_1 - X_2 - 3X_3 \geq 12$$

$5X_1 + 0.X_2 - 6X_3 \leq 13$

$X_1, X_2, X_3 \geq 0$

Dual : Let w_1, w_2, w_3 be the dual variables.

$\text{Min}(Z_d) = 8w_1 + 12w_2 + 13w_3$

Subject to

$4w_1 - 8w_2 + 5w_3 \geq 3$

$-w_1 - w_2 + 0.w_3 \geq -1$

$0.w_1 - 3.w_2 - 6.w_3 \geq 1$

Finally

$\text{Min}(Z_d) = 8w_1 + 12w_2 + 13w_3$

Subject to

$4w_1 - 8w_2 + 5w_3 \geq 3$

$-w_1 - w_2 \geq -1$

$-3.w_2 - 6.w_3 \geq 1$

$w_1, w_2 \geq 0$

Example 2 : Write the dual of the following LPP.

$\text{Min}(Z) = 2X_2 + 5X_3$

Subject to

$X_1 + X_2 \geq 2$

$2X_1 + X_2 + 6X_3 \leq 6$

$X_1 - X_2 + 3X_3 = 4$

$X_1, X_2, X_3 \geq 0$

Solution : Express the problem into the standard form of the primal.

$\text{Min}(Zp) = 0.X_1 + 2X_2 + 5X_3$

Subject to

$$X_1 + X_2 + 0.\ X_3 \geq 2$$
$$-2\ X_1 + X_2 - 6\ X_3 \geq 6$$
$$X_1 - X_2 + 3\ X_3 \leq 4$$
$$X_1 - X_2 + 3\ X_3 \geq 4$$
$$X_1, X_2, X_3 \geq 0$$

Again rearranging the constraints.

Min (Zp) = $0.\ X_1 + 2\ X_2 + 5\ X_3$

Subject to

$$X_1 + X_2 + 0.\ X_3 \geq 2$$
$$-2\ X_1 - X_2 - 6\ X_3 \geq 6$$
$$-X_1 + X_2 - 3\ X_3 \geq -4$$
$$X_1 - X_2 + 3\ X_3 \geq 4$$
$$X_1, X_2, X_3 \geq 0$$

Dual : Since there are four constraints in the primal, we have four variables in the dual namely w_1, w_2, w_3', w_3''.

Max (Zd) = $2\ w_1 + 6\ w_2 + 4\ w_3' - 4w_3''$

Subject to

$$w_1 - 2w_2 + w'_3 - w''_3 \leq 0$$
$$w_1 - w_2 - w'_3 + w''_3 \leq 2$$
$$w_1 - 6\ w_2 + 3\ w'_3 - 3w''_3 \leq 5$$
$$w_1, w_2, w'_3, w''_3 \geq 0$$

Now

Max (Z_d) = $2\ w_1 + 6\ w_2 + 4\ (w'_3 - w''_3)$

Subject to

$$w_1 - 2w_2 + (w'_3 - w''_3) \leq 0$$
$$w_1 - w_2 - (w'_3 - w''_3) \leq 2$$

$w_1 - 6 w_2 + 3 (w'_3 - w''_3) \leq 5$

$w_1 , w_2, w'_3 , w''_3 \geq 0$

Finally

Let $w_3 = w_3' - w_3''$

$\text{Max } (Z_D) = 2 w_1 + 6w_2 + 4w_3$

$w_1 - 2w_2 + w_3 \leq 0$

$w_1 - w_2 - w_3 \leq 2$

$-6w_2 + 3w_3 \leq 5$

$w_1, w_2 \geq 0$, w_3 is restricted.

Example 3 : Find the dual of the following LPP.

$\text{Max } (Z) = X + 2Y$

Subject to

$2 X + 3 Y \geq 4$

$3 X + 4 Y = 5$

$X \geq 0$, and Y is unrestricted.

Solution :

Since the variable Y is unrestricted, it can be expressed as $Y = Y' - Y''$

Where $Y' , Y'' \geq 0$.

Now $\text{Max } (Z) = X + 2(Y' - Y'')$

Subject to

$2 X + 3 (Y' - Y'') \geq 4$

$3 X + 4 (Y'-Y'') = 5$

Again $\text{Max } (Z) = X + 2Y' - 2 Y''$

Subject to

$2X + 3Y' + 3Y'' \geq 4$

$3X + 4Y' - 4Y'' = 5$

Now express the problem into the standard form of the Primal.

Max (Z) = $X + 2Y' - 2Y''$

Subject to

$-2X - 3Y' + 3Y'' \leq -4$

$3X + 4Y' - 4Y'' \leq 5$

$-3X - 4Y' + 4Y'' \leq -5$

Max (Z) = $X + 2Y' - 2Y''$

Subject to

$-2X - 3Y' + 3Y'' \leq -4$

$3X + 4Y' - 4Y'' \leq 5$

$-3X - 4Y' + 4Y'' \leq -5$

Dual : Since there are three constraints in the primal, thus there are three variable in the dual which are w_1, w'_2, w''_2.

Mi n (Zd) = $-4w_1 + 5w'_2 - 5w''_2$

Subject to

$-2w_1 + 3w'_2 - 3w''_2 \geq 1$

$-3w_1 + 4w'_2 - 4w''_2 \geq 2$

$3w_1 - 4w'_2 + 4w''_2 \geq -2$

Then the dual is

Min (Zd) = $-4w_1 + 5(w'_2 - w''_2)$

Subject to

$-2w_1 + 3(w'_2 - w''_2) \geq 1$

$-3w_1 + 4(w'_2 - w''_2) \geq 2$

$3w_1 - 4(w'_2 - w''_2) \geq -2$

Now let $w_2 = (w'_2 - w''_2)$

Mi n (Zd) = $-4 w_1 + 5 w_2$

Subject to

$-2 w_1 + 3 w_2 \geq 1$

$-3 w_1 + 4 w_2 \geq 2$

$3 w_1 - 4 w_2 \geq -2$

Again

Min (Z) = $-4w_1 + 5w_2$

Subject to

$-2w_1 + 3w_2 \geq 1$

$-3w_1 + 4w_2 \geq 2$

$-2w_1 + 4w_2 \leq 2$

Finally

Mi n $(Z_d) = -4 w_1 + 5 w_2$

Subject to

$-2 w_1 + 3 w_2 \geq 1$

$3w_1 + 4 w_2 = 2$

$w_1 \geq 0$, w_2 is unrestricted.

Properties of Duality

1. The dual of the dual is primal.
2. If one is maximization problem then the other is a minimization one.
3. The necessary and sufficient condition for any LPP and its dual to have an optimal solution is that both must have feasible solution.
4. Fundamental duality theorem states that if either the primal or dual problem has a finite optimal solution, then the other problem also has a finite optimal values of the objective function in both the problem are same i.e Max

(Z) = Min (Z′). The solution of the other problem can be read from the (Cj – Zj) row below the column of slack, and artificial variables.

5. Existence theorem states that, if either problem has an unbounded solution then the other problem has no feasible solution.

Solution of the Dual Problem:

(By using Big-M Method)

Example 1 : Find the Maximum of $Z = 6X + 8Y$

Subject to $5X + 2Y \le 20$

$X + 2Y \ge 10$

$X, Y \ge 0$ by solving its dual problem.

Solution:

Step 1. The dual of the problem is given below. As there are two constraints in the primal, we have two dual variables namely w_1, w_2.

$\text{Min}(Z') = 20w_1 + 10w_2$

Subject to

$5w_1 + w_2 \ge 6$

$2w_1 + 2w_2 \ge 8$

$w_1, w_2 = 0$

Step 2. We solve the dual problem using Big- m method.

$\text{Max}(Z') = -20w_1 - 10w_2 + 0.S_1 + 0.S_2 - M.A_1 - M.A_2$

Subject to

$5w_1 + w_2 - S_1 + A_1 = 6$

$2w_1 + 2w_2 - S_2 + A_2 = 8$

CB	B_m	X_B	w_1 (-20)	w_2 (-10)	S_1 (0)	S_2 (0)	A_1 (-M)	A_2 (-M)	Min ratio
-M	A1	6	(5)	1	-1	0	1	0	6/5=1.02 ←
-M	A2	8	2	2	0	-1	0	1	8/2=4
Z=-14M		Zj=	-7M	-3M	M	M	-M	-M	
		Cj-Zj =	(-20+7M) ↑	(-10+3M)	-M	-M	M	M	
-20	W1	6/5	1	1/5	-1/5	0	-	0	6
-M	A2	28/5	0	(8/5)	2/5	-1/5	-	1	28/8 ←
Z= - 28/5M-24		Zj=	-20	(-4 – 8/5M)	(-4-2/5M)	M	-	- M	
		Cj-Zj=	0	(- 6 + 8/5 M) ↑	(4+2/5M)	M	-	0	
-20	W1	1/2	1	0	1/4	1/8	-	-	
-10	W2	7/2	0	1	1/4	-5/8	-	-	
Z=-45		Zj=	-20	-10	5/2	15/4	-	-	
		Cj- Zj=	0	0	- 5/2	-15/4	-	-	

Since all $(C_j - Z_j) \leq 0$ the solution is optimum. Therefore, the optimum solution of the dual is $w_1 = 1/2$, $w_2 = 7/2$, Min $(Z') = -45$

The optimum solution of the primal is

$X=5/2$ $Y= 15/4$, Max $(Z) = 6 \times 5/2 + 8 \times 15/4 = 45$

4.5 Two Phase Method:

The two Phase method is also a method to solve LPP with mixed constraints (≤ , ≤ or =). In this method, we involve some artificial variable like Big-M method. The solution is obtained in two phases.

Phase I .

Step 1. Construction of an auxiliary LPP.

In this phase, we construct an auxiliary LPP which leads to a final simplex table containing a basic feasible solution to the original problem.

(a) To make a new objective function by assigning a cost (-1) to each artificial variable and a cost (0) to all other variables.

(b) Write down the auxiliary LPP in which the new objective function has to be maximized subject to the given constraints.

Step 2. Solution of the auxiliary LPP.

Solve the auxiliary LPP by using the simplex method until either of the following three cases arise. **(For all cases $Cj - Zj \leq 0$)**

Case 1. Max (Z^*) < 0 and, at least one artificial basic variable appear in basis at positive value.

Case 2. Max (Z^*) = 0 and, at least one artificial basic variable in the basis at zero value.

Case 3. Max (Z^*) = 0 and, no artificial variable appears in the basis.

In case (i), given LPP does not posses any feasible solution, where as in case (ii) and (iii) we go to the **Phase II.**

Phase II.

Step 1. Construction of the original LPP table.

Use the optimum basic feasible solution of Phase I as a starting solution for original LPP. Assign the actual cost to the variable in the objective function and a zero cost to every artificial variable at basis. Delete the artificial variable of column from the table which is eliminated from the basis at Phase I.

Step 2. Solution of original LPP.

Solve the original LPP by using simplex method till an optimum basic feasible is obtained or till there is an indication of unbounded solution.

Example 1: Use two- phase simplex method to solve

Max (Z) = 5 X1 + 3 X2

Subject to

$2X1 + X2 \leq 1$

$X1 + 4X2 \geq 6$

$X1, X2 \geq 0$

Solution:

Phase 1.

Step 1. Construction of an auxiliary LPP.

$\text{Max}(Z^*) = 0.X_1 + 0.X_2 + 0.S_1 + 0.S_2 - 1.A_1$

Subject to

$2X_1 + X_2 + S_1 = 1$

$X_1 + 4X_2 - S_2 + A_1 = 6$

Step. 2 Solve the auxiliary LPP by using the simplex method.

		C_j	0	0	0	0	-1	
C_b	b_i	X_b	X_1	X_2	S_1	S_2	A_1	Min Ratio
0	S1	1	2	(1)	1	0	0	1/1=1 ←
-1	A1	6	1	4	0	-1	1	6/1=6
Z= -6		Z_j=	-1	-4	0	1	-1	
		$C_j - Z_j$	1	4 ↑	0	1	-1	
0	X2	1	2	1	1	0	0	
-1	A1	2	-7	0	-4	-1	1	
Z= -2		Z_j=	7	0	4	1	-1	
		$C_j - Z_j$	-7	0	-4	-1	0	

Since all $C_j - Z_j \leq 0$, an optimum feasible solution to the auxiliary LPP is obtained. In this case, Max $(Z^*) < 0$, and an artificial variable (A_1) is in the basis at positive value. Thus, the original LPP does not posses any feasible solution.

Example 2: Solve the following LPP by using two Phase method.

$\text{Max}(Z) = 5X_1 - 4X_2 + 3X_3$

Subject to

$2X_1 + X_2 - 6X_3 = 20$

$6X_1 + 5X_2 + 10X_3 \leq 76$

$8X_1 - 3X_2 + 6X_3 \leq 50$

$X_1, X_2, X_3 \geq 0$

Solution: Phase I.

Step 1. Construction of an auxiliary LPP.

Max $(Z^*) = 0 . X_1 + 0. X_2 + 0.X_3 + 0.S_1 + 0. S_2 - A_1$

Subject to

$2X_1 + X_2 - 6X_3 + A_1 = 20$

$6X_1 + 5X_2 + 10X_3 + S_1 = 76$

$8X_1 - 3X_2 + 6X_3 + S_2 = 50$

$X_1, X_2, X_3, S_1, S_2, A_1 \geq 0$

Step 2. Solution of an auxiliary LPP.

C_j 0 0 0 -1 0 0

C_b	b_i	X_b	X_1	X_2	X_3	A_1	S_1	S_2	Min Ratio
-1	A_1	20	2	-1	-6	1	0	0	20/2=10
0	S_1	76	6	5	10	0	1	0	76/6=12.66
0	S_2	50	(8)	-3	6	0	0	1	50/8=6.25 ←
Z= -20		Z_j=	-2	-1	6	-1	0	0	
		$C_j - Z_j$	2 ↑	1	-6	0	0	0	
-1	A_1	15/2	0	(7/4)	-15/2	1	0	-1/4	30/7
0	S_1	77/2	0	29/4	11/2	0	1	-3/4	154/29
0	X_1	25/4	1	-3/8	3/4	0	0	1/8	--
Z= -		Z_j=	0	-7/4	15/2	-1	0	1/4	
15/2		C_j- Z_j	0	7/4 ↑	-15/2	0	0	-1/4	

Since all $C_j - Z_j \leq 0$ an optimum solution to the auxiliary LPP has been obtained. Also Max (Z*) = 0 with no artificial variable in the basis.

C_j			0	0	0	-1	0	0
C_b	b_i	X_b	X_1	X_2	X_3	A_1	S_1	S_2
0	X_2	30/7	0	1	-30/7	4/7	0	-1/7
0	S_1	52/7	0	1	256/7	-29/7	1	2/7
0	X_1	55/7	1	0	-6/7	3/4	0	1/14
Z= 0		Zj = Cj - Zj	0	0	0	0	0	0
			0	0	0	-1	0	0

Phase II.

C_b	b_i	X_b	X_1	X_2	X_3	S_1	S_2
0	X_2	30/7	0	1	-30/7	0	-1/7
0	S_1	52/7	0	1	256/7	1	2/7
0	X_1	55/7	1	0	-6/7	0	1/14
Z=		Z_j=	5	-4	90/7	0	13/14
155/7		$C_j - Z_j$	0	0	- 69/7	0	- 13/14

Since all $C_j - Z_j \leq 0$ an optimum basic feasible solution has been reached. Hence , an optimum feasible solution to the given LPP is $X_1 = 55/7$, $X_2 = 30/7$,

and Max (z)= 155/7.

4.6 Degeneracy in Simplex Method:

A B.F.S. of a Simplex method is said to be degenerate B.F.S.

(i) If at least one of the basic variable is zero. And

(ii) At any iteration of the simplex method more than one variable is eligible to leave the basis and hence the next simplex iteration produces a degenerate solution in which at least one basic variable is zero. This concept is known as tie.

Conditions of degeneracy in Simplex Method:

In a Simplex method, the degeneracy may appear in the following two ways.

(i) The degeneracy appear in a simplex method at the first iteration when some basic variable (b_i) is zero.

(ii) If none of the basic variable is zero at any iteration and the minimum ratio is not unique. (There is tie in minimum ratio.)

Methods to resolve Degeneracy :

Step 1. First find out the rows for which the minimum non - negative ratio is the same (tie).

Step 2. Now rearranges the columns of the usual simplex table so that identity matrix comes first in proper order.

Step 3. Find the minimum ratio, by dividing the elements of first column of the unit matrix with the corresponding element of a key column.

$$\text{Now Minimum Ratio} = \frac{\text{(Element of the first column of the unit Matrix.)}}{\text{(Corresponding element of key column)}}$$

Step 4. If the minimum ratio is not unique, then find the minimum ratio by dividing the elements of second column of the unit matrix with the corresponding element of a key column.

$$\text{Now Minimum Ratio} = \frac{\text{(Element of the second column of the unit Matrix)}}{\text{(Corresponding element of key column)}}$$

Step 5. If the minimum ratio is not unique, then the above step is repeated till the minimum ratio is obtained so as to resolve the degeneracy.

4.7 Practice Problem

Example 1. Solve the L.P.P

Max (Z)= 2. $X_1 + X_2$

Subject to $4X_1 + 3X_2 \leq 12$

$4X_1 + X_2 \leq 8$

$4X_1 - X_2 \leq 8$

$X_1, X_2 \geq 0$

Solution :

Step 1. Express the problem into the standard form.

Max (Z) = 2 X1 + X2 + 0.S1 + 0.S2 + 0. S3

s.t

4 X1 + 3 X2 + S1 =12

4 X1 + X2 + S2 = 8

4X1 – X2 + S3 = 8

Step 3. Find initial basic feasible solution.

1st table

		Cj	2	1	0	0	0	
Cb	bi	Xb	X1	X2	S1	S2	S3	Min. Ratio
0	S1	12	4	3	1	0	0	12/4=3
0	S2	8	4	1	0	1	0	8/4=2 } Tie
0	S3	8	4	-1	0	0	1	8/4=2 }
Z=0		Zj=	0	0	0	0	0	
		Cj – Zj=	2 ↑	1	0	0	0	

Since the minimum ratio is not unique. This is an indication of degeneracy in the given LPP. Thus, we have to resolve degeneracy for solving the problem.

Now rearrange the simplex table so that the identity matrix comes first.

2nd table

Cb	bi	Xb	S1	S2	S3	X1	X2	Min. Ratio
0	S1	12	1	0	0	4	3	--
0	S2	8	0	1	0	4	1	1/4
0	S3	8	0	0	1	(4)	-1	0 ← Key row
Z=0		Zj=	0	0	0	0	0	
		Cj – Zj=	0	0	0	2	1	

↑ Key column (X1)

3rd table

		Cj	0	0	0	2	1	
Cb	bi	Xb	S1	S2	S3	X1	X2	Min. Ratio
0	S1	4	1	0	-1	0	4	1
0	S2	0	0	1	-1	0	(2)	0 (Min) ← (key row)
2	X1	2	0	0	1/4	1	-1/4	negative
Z=4		Zj=	0	0	1/2	2	-2/4	
		Cj – Zj=	0	0	-1/2	0	3/2	

↑ Key column (X2)

4th table

		Cj	0	0	0	2	1	
Cb	bi	Xb	S1	S2	S3	X1	X2	Min. Ratio
0	S1	4	1	-2	(1)	0	0	4 ← (key row)
1	X2	0	0	1/2	-1/2	0	1	Negative
2	X1	2	0	1/8	1/8	1	0	16
Z=4		Zj=	0	3/4	-1/4	2	1	
		Cj – Zj=	0	-3/4	1/4	0	0	

↑ Key column (S3)

5th table

		Cj	0	0	0	2	1	
Cb	bi	Xb	S1	S2	S3	X1	X2	Min. Ratio
0	S1	4	1	-2	1	0	0	-
1	X2	2	1/2	-1/2	0	0	1	-
2	X1	3/2	-1/8	1/8	0	1	0	-
Z=5		Zj=	1/4	1/4	0	2	1	
		Cj – Zj=	-1/4	-1/4	0	0	0	

Since all Cj- Zj ≤ 0 therefore the solution is optimal.

Optimal solution is X1 = 3/2 , X2 = 2 and Max (Z) = 5.

Example 2: Solve the following LPP with the help of simplex method.

Max (Z) = 3 X1 + 9 X2

Subject to

X1 + 4 X2 ≤ 8

X1 + 2 X2 ≤ 4

X1 , X2 ≥ 0

Solution :

Step 1. Express the problem into the standard form.

Max (Z) = 3 X1 + 9 X2 + 0. S1 + 0. S2

Subject to

X1 + 4 X2 + S1 = 8

X1 + 2 X2 + S2 = 4

Step 2. Find the initial basic feasible solution.

1st table

		Cj	3	9	0	0	
C_b	b_i	X_b	X_1	X_2	S_1	S_2	Min. Ratio
0	S1	9	1	4	1	0	8/4=2 } tie
0	S2	4	1	2	0	1	4/2=2 } tie
Z=0		Zj=	0	0	0	0	
		Cj- Zj=	3	9	0	0	

↑ Key column

In the above simplex table, the minimum ratio is not unique. It represents the degeneracy in the given LPP.

Rearrange the above simplex table so that the identity matrix comes first in proper order.

		Cj	0	0	3	9	
C_b	b_i	X_b	S_1	S_2	X_1	X_2	Min. Ratio
0	S1	8	1	0	1	4	1/4=2
0	S2	4	0	1	1	(2)	0/2=0 ←
Z=0		Zj=	0	0	0	0	
		Cj- Zj=	0	0	3	9 ↑	

Entering Variable= X_2 , Leaving Variable= S_2

		Cj	0	0	3	9	
C_b	b_i	X_b	S_1	S_2	X_1	X_2	Min. Ratio
0	S1	0	1	-2	-1	0	-
9	S2	2	0	1/2	1/2	1	-
Z=18		Zj=	0	9/2	9/2	9	
		Cj- Zj=	0	-9/2	-3/2	0	

Since all Cj - Zj ≤ 0 , the solution is optimum. The optimum solution is X1 = 0 , X2 = 2 , Max (Z)= 18.

Practice Problem

1. What is simplex? Describe the simplex method of solving linear programming problem?
2. Explain the purpose and procedure of the simplex method.
3. Define slack and surplus variables in a linear programming.
4. What are artificial variables and its use in linear programming?
5. What conditions must exist in a simplex table to establish the existence of an alternative solution? No feasible solution? Unbounded solution? Degeneracy?
6. How the graphical and simplex methods of solving LP problems do differ?
7. How do the maximization and minimization problems differ when applying the simplex method?
8. What do mean by an optimal basic feasible solution to a linear programming problem?
9. What is the reason behind the use of the minimum ratio test in selecting the key row?
10. Describe the tow phase method of solving an LP problem with artificial variables.
11. Give the computational procedure for simplex method in linear programming.
12. Write short notes on Two phase method.
13. Explain the Big-M method in linear programming.
14. Explain the term degeneracy in the context of L.P.P.
15. Discuss a method to resolve the degeneracy in L.P.P.
16. What is duality in linear programming?
17. Write the short notes on following?
    (a) Unbounded Solution
    (b) Infeasible Solution
    (c) Dual and Primal

(d) Basic feasible solution

(e) Degenerate problem

18. Solve the following problems by simplex method.

(a) Max (Z) = $2X_1 + 4X_2 + X_3$

Subject to

$X_1 + 2X_2 = 4$

$2X_1 + X_2 = 3$

$X_2 + 4X_3 = 3$

$X_1, X_2, X_3 = 0$

(b) Max (z) = $5X_1 + 3X_2$

Subject to

$X_1 + X_2 = 2$

$5X_1 + 2X_2 = 10$

$3X_1 + 8X_2 = 12$

$X_1, X_2 = 0$

(c) Max (z) = $5X_1 + 3X_2$

Subject to

$3X_1 + 5X_2 = 15$

$5X_1 + 2X_2 = 10$

$X_1, X_2 = 0$

(d) Max (z) = $3X_1 - X_2$

Subject to

$2X_1 + X_2 = 2$

$X_1 + 3X_2 = 3$

$X_2 = 4$

$X_1, X_2 = 0$

19. Solve the following LPP

(a) Max (Z) =3 X_1 + 2 X_2

Subject to

$X_1 + X_2 = 4$

$X_1 - X_2 = 2$

$X_1, X_2 = 0$

(b) Max (z) = 5 X1 + 3 X2

Subject to

$X_1 + X_2 = 2$

$5X_1 + 2X_2 = 10$

$3X_1 + 8X_2 = 12$

$X_1, X_2 = 0$

(c) Max (Z) = $X_1 + X_2 + X_3$

Subject to

$4X_1 + 5X_2 + 3X_3 = 15$

$10X_1 + 7X_2 + X_3 = 12$

$X_1, X_2, X_3 = 0$

20. A company makes two products A and B. Each unit of product A requires twice as much labour time as the product B. If all the units are of product B, the company can produce a total of 500 units a day. The market limits daily sales of product A and B 150 and 250 units respectively. The profit per unit of A is Rs 8 and per unit of B is Rs 4. Determine optimal product mix to maximize the net profit of company.

21. Use penalty method to solve following LPP.

(a) Min (Z) = 2 X_1 + X_2

Subject to

$3X_1 + X_2 = 3$

$4X_1 + 3X_2 = 6$

$X_1 + 2X_2 = 3$

$X_1, X_2 = 0$

[Ans. $X_1 = 15$, $X_2 = 5/4$ and Min(Z)=205]

(b) Max (Z) = $2X_1 + 3X_2 + 5X_3$

Subject to

$3X_1 + 10X_2 + 5X_3 = 15$

$33X_1 - 10X_2 + 9X_3 = 33$

$X_1 + 2X_2 + X_3 = 4$

$X_1, X_2, X_3 = 0$

[Ans. No Solution]

(c) Max (Z) = $2X_1 + 4X_2 + X_3$

Subject to

$X_1 - 2X_2 - X_3 = 5$

$2X_1 - X_2 + 2X_3 - 2$

$-X_1 + 2X_2 + 2X_3 = 1$

$X_1, X_2, X_3 = 0$

[Ans. Unbounded Solution]

22. Use Two -Phase method to solve the following LPP.

(a) Min (Z) = $-2X_1 - X_2$

Subject to

$X_1 + X_2 = 2$

$X_1 + X_2 = 4$

$X_1, X_2 = 0$

[Ans. Min (Z)= -8 , $X_1 = 4$, $X_2 = 0$]

(b) Max (Z) = $2X_1 + X_2 + X_3$

Subject to

$4X_1 + 6X_2 + 3X_3 = 8$

$3X_1 - 6X_2 - 4X_3 = 1$

$2X_1 + 3X_2 - 5X_3 = 4$

$X_1, X_2, X_3 = 0$

[Ans. Max (Z) = 64/21, X_1= 9/7, X_2=10/2, X_3=0]

23. Degenerate Problem

(a) Max (z) = $2X_1 + 3X_2 + 10X_3$

Subject to

$X_1 + 2X_3 = 0$

$X_1 + X_3 = 1$

$X_1, X_2, X_3 = 0$

[Max (Z)= 3 , X_1=0 , X_2 =1 , X_3=0]

(b) Max (Z) = $X_1 + 2X_2 + X_3$

Subject to

$2X_1 + X_2 - X_3 = 2$

$-2X_1 + X_2 - 5X_3 = -6$

$4X_1 + X_2 + X_3 = 6$

$X_1, X_2, X_3 = 0$

[Max (Z) =10 , X_1=0, X_2=4,X_3=2]

24. Dual Problem

(a) Apply the principle of duality to solve the LPP.

Max (Z) = $3X_1 + 2X_2$

Subject to

$X_1 + X_2 = 1$

$X_1 + X_2 = 7$

$X_1 + 2X_2 = 10$

$X_2 = 3$

$X_1, X_2 = 0$

[Ans. $X_1 = 7$, $X_2=0$, Max (Z)=21]

(b) Write the dual of the following LPP.

Min (Z) = $X_1 - X_2 + X_3$

Subject to

$X_1 - X_3 = 4$

$X_1 - X_2 + 2X_3 = 3$

$X_1, X_2, X_3 = 0$

[Ans. Max (Z') = $4W_1 + 3W_2$

Subject to

$W_1 + W_2 = 1$

$0. W_1 - W_2 = -1$

$-W_1 + 2W_2 = 1$

$W_1, W_2 = 0$]

(c) Write the dual of the following LPP and solve it.

Max (Z) = $4X_1 + 2X_2$

Subject to

$X_1 + X_2 = 3$

$X_1 - X_2 = 2$

$X_1, X_2 = 0$

[Ans. Unbounded solution.]

25. Obtain the dual of the following LPP.

(a) Max (Z)= $X_1 - X_2 + 3X_3$

Subject to

$X_1 + X_2 + X_3 = 10$

$2X_1 - X_3 = 2$

$2X_1 - 2X_2 + 3X_3 = 6$

$X_1, X_2, X_3 = 0$

[Ans. Min $(Z') = 10W_1 + 2W_2 + 6W_3$

Subject to

$W_1 + 2W_2 + 2W_3 = 1$

$W_1 + 2W_3 = -1$

$W_1 - W_2 + 3W_3 = 3$

$W_1, W_2, W_3 = 0$]

(b) Max $(Z) = 3X_1 + X_2 + 2X_3 - X_4$

Subject to

$2X_1 - X_2 + 3X_3 + X_4 = 1$

$X_1 + X_2 - X_3 + X_4 = 3$

$X_1, X_2, X_3 = 0$

And X4 is unrestricted.

[Ans. Min $(Z') = W_1 + 3W_2$

Subject to

$2W_1 + W_2 = 3$

$-W_1 + W_2 = 1$]

Objective Question:

1. The constraints of Maximization problem are of -
   (a) greater than or equal to type
   (b) less than or equal type
   (c) Less than type
   (d) Greater than type

2. The slack variables indicate –
   (a) excess resource available
   (b) shortage of resource available
   (c) Nil resource
   (d) Idle resource
3. To convert = type of inequality in to equations we have to

(a) assume them to be equations

(b) add surplus variables

(c) subtract slack variables

(d) Add slack variables

4. To convert = type of inequality in to equations we have to
   (a) assume them to be equations
   (b) add surplus variables
   (c) subtract slack variables
   (d) Add slack variables
5. The key row indicates
   (a) Outgoing variable
   (b) Incoming variable
   (c) Slack variable
   (d) Surplus variable
6. The key column indicates
   (a) outgoing variable
   (b) Incoming Variable
   (c) Independent Variable
   (d) Dependent variable
7. Dual of a Dual is
   (a) Primal
   (b) Dual
   (c) Prima Primal
   (d) Duo Primal

8. Primal of a Primal is
   (a) Primal
   (b) Dual
   (c) Prima Primal
   (d) Duo primal

9. Dual of a Dual of Dual is
   (a) dual
   (b) Primal
   (c) Double dual
   (d) Single dual

10. Primal of a Dual is
   (a) dual
   (a) Primal
   (b) Double dual
   (c) Single dual

11. If Dual has a solution, then the primal will
   (a) Not have a solution
   (b) Have only basic feasible solution
   (c) Have a solution
   (d) None of the above

[Ans. 1(b) 2 (d) 3(d) 4 (b) 5 (a) 6 (b) 7 (a) 8 (a) 9 (b) 10 (b) 11(a)]

Chapter **5**

Transportation Problem

Course outline

5.1 Introduction

5.2 Definition

5.3 Mathematical form of Transportation problem

5.4 Basic term used in Transportation Problem

5.5 To find initial basic feasible solution

(1) North West Corner Method

(2) Least Cost Method

(3) Vogel's Approximation Method

5.6 To find optimal solution

(1) MODI Method

5.7 Unbalance problem

5.8 Degenerate problem

5.9 Practice Problem

5.1 Introduction:

The transportation problem is a special case of LPP in which the objective is to transport a homogeneous commodity from various origins to different destinations at a total minimum cost.

5.2 Definition:

The transportation problem can be defined as follows. Suppose that the factories F_i(i=1,2,3…..m) called the origins or sources produce the non-negative quantities a_i(i=1,2,….m) of the product and the non-negative quantities b_j(j=1,2…..n) of the same are required at other n places ,called the destinations such that the total quantity produced is equal to the total quantity required. i.e.

$$\sum_{i=1}^{m} a_i = \sum_{j=1}^{n} b_j$$

Also suppose that C_{ij} is the cost of transportation of a unit from the ith . Then the problem is to determine $x_{ij,}$ the quantity transported from the ith source to the jth destination, in such a way that the **total transportation cost**

$$\sum_{i=1}^{m} \sum_{j=1}^{n} C_{ij} \; X_{ij} \quad \textbf{is minimized.}$$

The Transportation Problem as described above can be represented by the following ways.

Sources/ Destinations	$W_1 W_2 \ldots\ldots W_j \ldots\ldots\ldots\ldots W_n$	Capacities (Supply)
F_1 F_2 ⋮ F_i ⋮ F_m	$C_{11}\ C_{12} \ldots\ldots C_{1j} \ldots\ldots\ldots\ldots C_{in}$ $C_{21}\ C_{22} \ldots\ldots C_{2j} \ldots\ldots\ldots\ldots C_{2n}$ $C_{i1}\ C_{i2} \ldots\ldots C_{ij} \ldots\ldots\ldots\ldots C_{in}$ $C_{m1}\ C_{m2} \ldots\ldots C_{mj} \ldots\ldots\ldots\ldots C_{mn}$	a_1 a_2 ⋮ a_i ⋮ a_m
Requirement (Demand)	$b_1\ \ b_2 \ldots\ldots\ldots b_j \ldots\ldots\ldots\ldots b_n$	$\sum_{i=1}^{n} a_i = \sum_{j=1}^{m} b_j$

5.3 Mathematical form of Transportation Problem

To find X_{ij} (i=1,2...m; j=1,2.....n) for which the total transportation cost

$$Z = \sum_{i=1}^{m} \sum_{j=1}^{n} C_{ij} X_{ij}$$ **is minimized.**

Subject to the restrictions

$$\sum_{i=1}^{n} x_{ij} = a_i \; i=1,2\ldots\ldots\ldots\ldots m$$

$$\sum_{i=1}^{n} x_{ij} = b_j \; ; j=1,2\ldots\ldots\ldots\ldots\ldots n.$$

The given transportation problem is said to be balanced if

$$\sum_{i=1}^{n} a_i = \sum_{j=1}^{m} b_j$$

(i.e Total demand is equal to the total supply)

5.4 Basic term used in Transportation Problem

There are few basic terms which are used in the transportation problem are given below.

1. A feasible solution (A.F.S.)

It is a set of non-negative individual allocation ($x_{ij} \geq 0$) which satisfies the row and column sum restrictions.

2. Basic Feasible solution (B.F.S.)

A feasible solution of m×n transportation problem is said to be a basic feasible solution if the total number of positive allocation x_{ij} is exactly equal to (m+n-1).

3. Optimal Solution:

A feasible solution (not necessarily basic) is said to be optimal if it minimizes the total transportation cost.

4. Non-Degenerate basic feasible solution:

A feasible solution of m×n transportation problem is said to be non degenerate B.F.S. if

(i) Total number of positive allocation is exactly equal to (m+n-1).

And

(ii) These allocations are in independent positions. The allocation are said to be in independent positions, if it is impossible to form a closed path. Closed path means by allowing horizontal and vertical lines and all corner cells are occupied. This means allocations make a loop.

Independent position

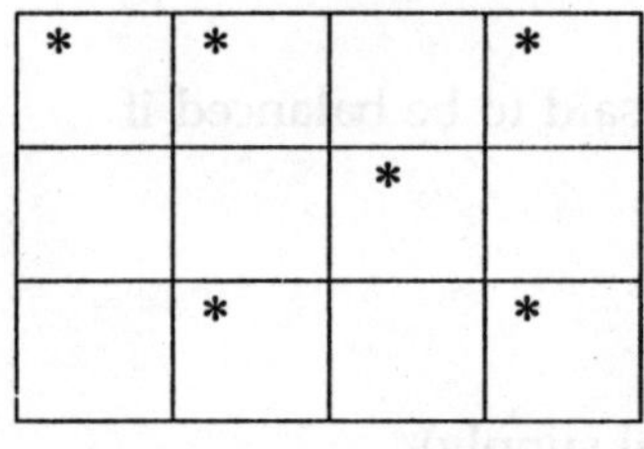

Non independent positions

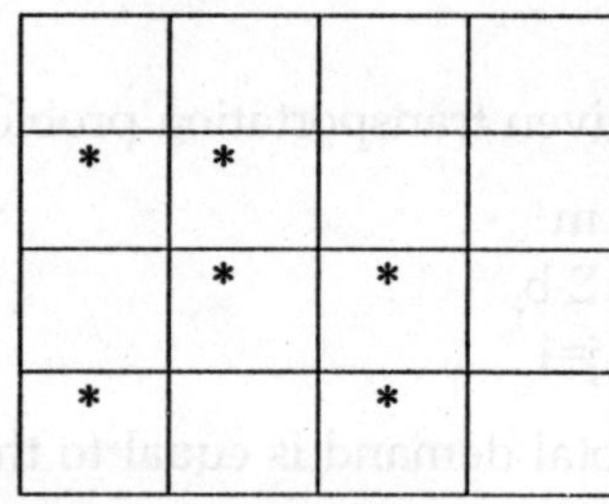

Closed path

5. Degenerate basic feasible solution

If a Basic Feasible Solution contains less than (m+n-1) non negative allocations, it is said to be degenerate.

Solution of Transportation Problem

We can solve the transportation problem with the help of following steps.

(a) To find an initial basic feasible solution

It can be obtained by using any one of the three methods.

(i) North-west Corner Rule (NWCR)

(ii) Least-Cost Method or Matrix Minima Method (LCM)

(iii) Vogel's approximation method (VAM)

VAM is better than other two methods, since the initial basic feasible solution obtained by this method is either optimal or very close to the optimal solution.

(b) To find the optimal solution by making successive improvements in initial basic feasible solutions by using any one method.
   (i) The stepping stone method
   (ii) The Modified distribution method (MODI method) or (U-V method)

5.5 To find initial basic feasible solution:

(i) North –West Corner Rule (NWC):

Step 1. Start with the cell (1,1) at the North- West Corner i.e. the top most left corner and allocate it maximum possible amount.

Step 2. Then move to the right hand cell (1,2) if there is any available quantity left otherwise move to the down (2,1) and allocate it maximum possible amount.

Step 3. Repeat the Step 2 again and continue until all the available quantity is exhausted.

Example 1: Obtain the initial basic feasible solution of a transportation problem whose cost and rim requirement table is given below.

Origin /Destination	D_1	D_2	D_3	Supply
O_1	2	7	4	5
O_2	3	3	1	8
O_3	5	4	7	7
O_4	1	6	2	14
Demand	7	9	18	**34**

Solution: Since $\Sigma a_i = \Sigma b_j$ then there exists a feasible solution. By using the NWC method, we obtained the initial basic feasible solution of the problem.

Origin /Destination	D_1	D_2	D_3	Supply
O_1	2 (5)	7	4	5, 0
O_2	3 (2)	3 (6)	1	8 , 6 , 0
O_3	5	4 (3)	7 (4)	7 , 4 , 0
O_4	1	6	2(14)	14, 0
Demand	7 2 0	9 3 0	18 14 0	34

Hence, we get the initial basic feasible solution to the given transportation problem i.e.

$X_{11}=5, X_{21}=2, X_{22}=6, X_{32}=3, X_{33}=4, X_{43}=14$

Total Cost = (2×5)+(3×2)+(3×6)+(4×3)+(7×4)+(2×14)

= Rs 102

(ii) Least cost Method (LCM):

Step 1. Determines the smallest cost in the cost matrix of the transportation table. Let it be C_{ij}. Allocate X_{ij}= min (a_i, b_j) in the cell (i,j).

Step 2. If $X_{ij} = a_i$ cross off the ith row of the transportation table and decrease b_j by a_i. Then go to step.3 or If $X_{ij} = b_j$ cross off the jth column of the transportation table and decreases a_i by b_j then go to step3. If $X_{ij}=a_i=b_j$ cross off either i^{th} row or j^{th} column but not both.

Step 3. Repeat step 1 and 2 for the resulting reduced transportation table until the entire rim requirement are satisfied.

Example: Determine an initial basic feasible solution for the following Transportation problem by using least cost method.

	W_1	W_2	W_3	W_4	Capacity
O_1	6	4	1	5	14
O_2	8	9	2	7	16
O_3	4	3	6	2	5
Requirement	6	10	15	4	35

Solution: Since demand is equal to supply ($\Sigma a_i = \Sigma b_j$), thus there exist a basic feasible solution. Thus the above problem can be solved with the help of using least cost method.

Step 1.

	W_1	W_2	W_3	W_4	Capacity
O_1	6	4	1 (14)	5	14, 0
O_2	8	9	2	7	16
O_3	4	3	6	2	5
Requirement	6	10	15 1	4	35

Step 2.

	W_1	W_2	W_3	W_4	Capacity
O_2	8	9	2 (1)	7	16, 15
O_3	4	3	6	2	5
Requirement	6	10	1 0	4	

Step 3.

	W_1	W_2	W_4	Capacity
O_2	8	9	7	15
O_3	4	3	2 (4)	5, 1
Requirement	6	10	4 0	

Step 4.

	W_1	W_2	Capacity
O_2	8	9	15
O_3	4	3 (1)	1 , 0
Requirement	6	10 9	

Step 5.

	W_1	W_2	Capacity
O_2	8 (6)	9 (9)	15, 0
Requirement	6 0	9 0	

The following table gives the initial basic feasible solution.

	W_1	W_2	W_3	W_4	Capacity
O_1	6	4	1 (14)	5	14
O_2	8 (6)	9 (9)	2 (1)	7	16
O_3	4	3 (1)	6	2 (4)	5
Requirements	6	10	15	4	

Hence, we get the initial basic feasible solution to the given transportation problem i.e.

$X_{13}= 14, X_{21}=6, X_{22}=9, X_{23}=1, X_{32}=1, X_{34}=4$

Total transportation cost = (1 x 14) + (8 x 6) + (9 x 9) + (2 x 1) + (3 x 1) + (2 x 4) = Rs.156

(iii) Vogel's Approximation method (VAM):

Step 1. Find the penalty cost, i.e. the difference between the smallest and next smallest costs in each row and column.

Step 2. Among the penalties as found in Step 1choose the maximum penalty if the maximum penalty is more than one (if there is a tie) choose any one arbitrarily.

Step 3. In the selected row or column as by Step 2 find out the cell having the least cost. Allocate to this cell as much as possible depending on the capacity and requirements.

Step 4. Delete the row or column, which is fully exhausted. Again compute the column and row penalties for the reduced transportation table and then go to the step 2. Repeat the procedure until the entire rim requirement are satisfied.

Example. Solve the transportation problem when the unit transportation costs, demand, supplies are as given below.

	Destination					
		D1	D2	D3	D4	Supply
Origins	O1	2	2	2	1	3
	O2	10	8	5	4	7
	O3	7	6	6	8	5
	Demand	4	3	4	4	15

Solution: Step 1 Since the total demand =the total supply . therefore the transportation problem is Balance.

	D1	D2	D3	D4	Supply	P1	P2	P3	P4	P5	P6
O1	2 (3)	2	2	1	3	1	-	-	-	-	-
O2	10	8	5 (3)	4 (4)	7	1	1	3 ←	-	-	-
O3	7 (1)	6 (3)	6 (1)	8	5	0	0	0	0	0	6 ←
Demand	4	3	4	4	15						
P1	5 ↑	4	4	3							
P2	3	2	1	4 ↑							
P3	3	2	1	-							
P4	7 ↑	6	6	-							
P5	-	6 ↑	6	-							
P6	-	-	6	-							

Since the number of occupied cell =m+n-1 and are also independent, there exist a non-degenerate basic feasible solution.

	D1	D2	D3	D4	Supply
O1	2 (3)	2	2	1	3
O2	10	8	5 (3)	4 (4)	7
O3	7 (1)	6 (3)	6 (1)	8	5
Demand	4	3	4	4	15

Finally the initial basic feasible solution is given as:

The initial transportation cost = (3 x 2) + (3 x 5) + (4 x 4) + (7 x 1) + (6 x 3) + (6 x 1) = Rs 68

5.6 To find the optimal solution:

After getting the initial basic feasible solution of a transportation problem, we test this solution for optimality. (i.e. we have to check the feasible solution obtained,minimizes the total transportation cost or not). For optimality test the initial basic feasible solution is equal to (m+n-1) allocations.

To perform this optimality test, we shall discuss the MODI method.

MODI Method:-

Step 1. Determine the initial basic feasible solution of a transportation problem by using any of the three methods.

Step 2. Find out a set of numbers u_i and v_j for each row and column satisfying $u_i+v_j=C_{ij}$ for each occupied cell. We have to assign a number '0' to any row or column having maximum numbers of allocations. If this maximum number of allocations is more than one, choose any one arbitrarily.

Step 3. For each empty (unoccupied) cell, we find the sum u_i and v_j.

Step 4. Find the cell evaluations $d_{ij}=C_{ij}-(u_i+v_j)$ for each unoccupied cell (i,j).

This step gives the following:

(i) If all $d_{ij} > 0$ then the solution is optimal and a unique solution exists.

(ii) If all $d_{ij} = 0$ then the solution is optimal, but an alternate solution exists.

(iii) If at least one $d_{ij} < 0$, the solution is not optimum. Then go to the next step.

Step 5. Selects that empty cell which has the most negative value d_{ij}. From this cell we draw a closed path by drawing horizontal and vertical lines, which the corner cells occupied. Assign (+) and (-) alternate and find the minimum allocation from the cell having (-) ive signs. This allocation should be added to the allocation having (+) sign and subtracted from the allocation having (-)ive sign.

Step 6. With the help of above step, we have one (or more) occupied cell as empty and one empty cell as occupied. For the new set of basic feasible allocations repeat from the step 2 till an optimum basic feasible solution is obtained.

Example.2 Solve the following Transportation Problem.

	To			Supply
	1	2	3	
	2	7	4	5
	3	3	1	8
	5	4	7	7
	1	6	2	14
Demand	7	9	18	34

Solution:

Step.1 By using VAM method we have the Initial Basic Feasible Solution.

2 (5)	7	4	5	u_1
3	3	1 (8)	8	u_2
5	4 (7)	7	7	u_3
1 (2)	6 (2)	2 (10)	14	u_4
7	9	18		
v_1	v_2	v_3	v_4	

The Total Transportation cost = 5 × 2 + 2 × 1 + 7 × 4 + 2×6+ 8 × 1 + 10 × 2 = Rs 80

Step.2 Now we determine a set of $\mathbf{u_i}$ and $\mathbf{v_j}$ for each occupied cell (i, j) ,$C_{ij} = u_i + v_j$. The maximum number of allocation contains in row u_4 therefore we assign $u_4 = 0$.

$C_{41} = 1 = u_4 + v_1$
$C_{42} = 6 = u_4 + v_2$
$C_{43} = 2 = u_4 + v_3$
$C_{11} = 2 = u_1 + v_1$
$C_{23} = 1 = u_2 + v_3$
$C_{32} = 7 = u_3 + v_2$

Therefore we have $v_1 = 1$, $v_2 = 6$, $v_3 = 2$, $u_1 = 1$, $u_2 = -1$, $u_3 = -2$

Step.3 Then we find the cell evaluations $d_{ij} = C_{ij} - (u_i + v_j)$ for each unoccupied cell (i, j).

$d_{12} = C_{12} - (u_1 + v_2) = 7 - (1 + 6) = 0$
$d_{13} = C_{13} - (u_1 + v_3) = 4 - (1 + 2) = 1$
$d_{21} = C_{21} - (u_2 + v_1) = 3 - (-1 + 1) = 3$
$d_{22} = C_{22} - (u_2 + v_2) = 3 - (-1 + 6) = -2$
$d_{31} = C_{31} - (u_3 + v_1) = 5 - (-2 + 1) = 6$
$d_{33} = C_{33} - (u_3 + v_3) = 7 - (-2 + 2) = 7$

Step.4. Since the value of d22 = - 2 < 0, so the solution is not optimum. Thus we give maximum allocation Ø to this cell and make necessary changes in other allocation by forming the following loop.

2 (5)	7	4	**5**
3	3 **d_{22}= -2** **(+ Ø)**	1 **(8-Ø)**	**8**
5	4 **(7)**	7	**7**
1 **(2)**	6 **(2- Ø)**	2 **(10+ Ø)**	**14**
7	**9**	**18**	

Since minimum allocation containing 2 – Ø therefore 2 – Ø =0 this implies that Ø =2.

Step.5 The final modified allocations are given below

2 (5)	7	4	**5**
3	3 (2)	1 (6)	**8**
5	4 (7)	7	**7**
1 (2)	6	2 (12)	**14**
7	**9**	**18**	

The transportation cost = 2 × 5 + 3 × 2 + 1 × 6 + 4 ×7 + 1 ×2 + 2 ×12 = Rs. 76.

Thus the solution of the given transportation problem is

From source 1 transport 5 units to destination 1.

From source 2 transport 2 and 6 units to destination 2 and 3 respectively.

From source 3 transport 7 units to destination 2.

From source 4 transport 2 and 12 units to destination 1 and 3 respectively.

And the total transportation cost = Rs. 76.

Example.3 Solve the following transportation problem.

5	3	7	3	8	5	**3**
5	6	12	5	7	11	**4**
2	1	3	4	8	2	**2**
9	6	10	5	10	9	**8**
3	**3**	**6**	**2**	**1**	**2**	**17**

Solution. By using VAM the initial basic feasible solution of the transportation problem is given by the following table.

5	3 (1)	7	3	8	5 (2)	3
5 (3)	6	12	5 (□)	7 (1)	11	4
2	1	3 (2)	4	8	2	2
9	6 (2)	10 (4)	5 (2)	10	9	8
3	3	6	2	1	2	17

Since the total number of allocation is 8 which is one less than m+n-1 = 9. Hence this solution is degenerate solution.

Now to resolve the degeneracy we allocate a small positive number □ the cell (2, 4) getting allocation at independent positions.

To test the solution for optimality

We have to apply MODI method for the optimality test

For each occupied cell we have to determine the set of numbers u_i and v_j s.t. $C_{ij} = u_i + v_j$

5	3 (1)	7	3	8	5 (2)	3	$u_1 = -3$
5 (3)	6	12	5 (□)	7 (1)	11	4	$u_2 = 0$
2	1	3 (2)	4	8	2	2	$u_3 = -7$
9	6 (2)	10 (4)	5 (2)	10	9	8	$u_4 = 0$
3	3	6	2	1	2	17	
$v_1=5$	$v_2=6$	$v_3=10$	$v_4=5$	$v_5=7$	$v_6=8$		

We determine the value d_{ij} for each unoccupied cell and we obtained the value dij = 0 , therefore the solution is optimum and an alternate solution exists.

Thus the minimum transportation cost =1 × 3 + 2 × 5 + 3 × 5 + 1 × 7 + 2 × 3 +2 × 6 +

4 × 10 + 2 × 5 = Rs. 103

5.7 Degenerate Transportation Problem:

If the number of non-negative independent allocations is less than m+n-1 ; where m is the number of destinations and n is the number of destinations (columns) there exists a degeneracy.

To resolve the degeneracy, we have to adopt the following steps.

(i) Among the empty cell , we choose an empty cell having the least cost which is of an independent position . if this cell is more than one , choose any one arbitrarily.

(ii) To the cell as chosen in step (i) we allocate a small positive quantity > 0. This cell is treated like other occupied cells and degeneracy is removed by adding one (more) accordingly.

After that adopt the steps involved in MODI method till an optimum solution is obtained.

Example1. A company has three plants A,B and C, 3 warehouses X, Y and Z. The number of units available at the plants is 60, 70, 80 and the demand at X, Y and Z are 50, 80, 80 respectively. The unit cost of the transportation is given in the following table.

	X	Y	Z
A	8	7	3
B	3	8	9
C	11	3	5

Find the allocation so that the transportation cost is minimum.

Solution:

	Warehouses			
PLANTS	X	Y	Z	Supply
A	8	7	3	60
B	3	8	9	70
C	11	3	5	80
Demand	50	80	80	210

Applying least cost method we have the initial basic feasible solution.

	X	Y	Z	Supply
A	8	7	3 (60)	60
B	3 (50)	8	9 (20)	70
C	11	3 (80)	5	80
Demand	50	80	80	210

The total number of occupied cell is 4 < m+n-1 = 5, resulting in degeneracy. To remove this degeneracy we add an empty cell (3,3) whose cost is minimum and is of independent position. Allocate to this cell a small quantity $\in > 0$. Hence, we have the initial solution in the following table.

	X	Y	Z	Supply
A	8	7	3 (60)	60
B	3 (50)	8	9 (20)	70
C	11	3 (80)	5 ($\in$)	80
Demand	50	80	80	210

The solution is given by

$X_{13} = 60$, $X_{21} = 50$, $X_{23} = 20$, $X_{32} = 80$, $X_{33} = \in$

The total transportation cost= $3 \times 60 + 3 \times 50 + 9 \times 20 + 3 \times 80 + 5 \times \in$

$= \text{Rs } 750 + 5 \in = \text{Rs } 750$

To find the Optimum solution (MODI method):

Let us determine a set of numbers u_i and v_j for each row and column with $C_{ij} = u_i + v_j$ for each occupied cell . To start with we give to 0 to the second row as it ha the maximum allocation.

	X	**Y**	**Z**	
A	**8**	**7**	**3** **(60)**	**u_1=0**
B	**3** **(50)**	**8**	**9** **(20)**	**u_2=0**
C	**11**	**3** **(80)**	**5** **($\in$)**	**u_3=2**
	v_1=3	**v_2=1**	**v_3=3**	

$C_{13} = u_1 + v_3 = 3$, $C_{21} = u_2 + v_1 = 3$, $C_{23} = u_2 + v_3 = 3$, $C_{32} = u_3 + v_2 = 3$, $C_{33} = u_3 + v_3 = 5$, $u_2 = 0$

On solving it we get the following.

$u_1 = 0$, $u_2 = 0$, $u_3 = 2$, $v_1 = 3$, $v_2 = 1$, $v_3 = 3$,

Now we find $D_{ij} = C_{ij} - (u_i + v_j)$ for each unoccupied cell.

$D_{11} = C_{11} - (u_1 + v_1) = 8 - (0+3) = 5$

$D_{12} = C_{12} - (u_1 + v_2) = 7 - (0+3) = 4$

$D_{22} = C_{22} - (u_2 + v_2) = 8 - (0+1) = 7$

$D_{31} = C_{31} - (u_3 + v_1) = 11 - (2+3) = 6$

Since all D_{ij} ³ 0, we have obtained a optimum solution.

The solution is given by

$X_{13} = 60$, $X_{21} = 50$, $X_{23} = 20$, $X_{32} = 80$, $X_{33} = \in$

The total transportation cost= $3 \times 60 + 3 \times 50 + 9 \times 20 + 3 \times 80 + 5 \times \in$
$= \text{Rs } 750 + 5 \in = \text{Rs } 750$

5.8 Unbalance Transportation Problem:

A transportation problem is said to be an unbalance transportation problem, if the total supply is not equal to the total demand i.e.

$$\sum_{i=1}^{m} a_i \neq \sum_{j=1}^{n} b_j$$

an unbalance transportation problem is converted into a balance transportation problem, by introducing a dummy row or column which will provide a surplus supply or demand. After that it is solved by the earlier methods.

Example.1 Plant the Production programme so as to minimize the total cost of transportation.

Plants	Ranchi	Delhi	Lucknow	Kanpur	Capacity
Bombay	90	90	100	100	200
Calcutta	50	70	130	85	100
Demand	75	100	100	30	

Solution:

Since the Total Demand is not equal to the Total Supply therefore it is a unbalance transportation problem. After balancing transportation problem we have the following.

Plants	Ranchi	Delhi	Lucknow	Kanpur	Capacity
Bombay	90	90	100	100	200
Calcutta	50	70	130	85	100
Dummy	0	0	0	0	5
Demand	75	100	100	30	305

By using Vogel's Approximation Method, we obtained the initial allocations as follows:

Plants	Ranchi	Delhi	Lucknow	Kanpur	Capacity
Bombay	90	90 (75)	100 (95)	100 (30)	200
Calcutta	50 (75)	70 (25)	130	85	100
Dummy	0	0	0 (5)	0	5
Demand	75	100	100	30	

To test the optimality of the solution, we use MODI's method and observe that the solution arrived at by VAM is optimal. The allocation in the dummy row for Lucknow indicates that there is surplus demand. The transportation cost according to this optimal works out to

Total cost = (90 × 75) + (100 × 95) + (100 × 30) + (50 × 75) + (70 × 25) + (0 × 25)

= Rs. 24,750

5.9 Practice Problem:

1. What do you mean by transportation problem?
2. Explain the term degeneracy in the context of transportation problem.
3. Describe the methods to obtained ban initial basic feasible solution for transportation problem?
4. Write the short notes on following-
   (i) Unbalance transportation problem
   (ii) Maximization transportation problem
   (iii) MODI Method
5. Define feasible solution, basic solution, degenerate solution, non-degenerate solution and optimal solution in transportation problem.
6. Give the mathematical formulation of a transportation problem.
7. Obtain the initial basic feasible solution of the following transportation problem using
   (i) NWCR (ii) Least cost method
   (iii) VAM

	A	B	C	Supply
1	2	7	4	5
2	3	3	1	8
3	5	4	7	7
4	1	6	2	14
Demand	7	9	18	34

8. Solve the following transportation problem

	1	2	3	Capacity
1	2	2	3	10
2	4	1	2	15
3	1	3	1	40
Demand	20	15	30	

9. Solve the following transportation problem

	A	B	C	D	Capacity
P	5	4	2	6	20
Q	8	3	5	7	30
R	5	9	4	6	50
Demand	10	40	20	30	100

10. A manufacturer wants to ship 8 loads of his product as shown below. The matrix gives the mileage from origin 0 to the destination

Demand	A	B	C	Available
X	50	30	220	1
Y	90	45	170	3
Z	250	200	50	4
Required	4	2	2	8

Shipping costs are Rs.10 per load mile. What shipping schedule should be used?

11. A textile firm has three factories F_1, F_2, F_3 and four warehouses w_1, w_2, w_3, w_4. The transportation costs, factory capacities and warehouse requirements are given in the following table:

	W_1	W_2	W_3	W_4	Capacity
F1	15	24	11	12	5000
F2	25	20	14	16	1000
F3	12	16	22	13	7000
Demand	3000	2500	3500	4000	

12. Solve the following Transportation problem to maximize the profit.

	A	B	C	D	Supply
1	40	25	22	33	100
2	44	35	30	30	30
3	38	38	28	30	70
Demand	40	20	60	30	

13. Solve the following transportation problem .

	A	B	C	D	Supply
1	11	20	7	8	50
2	21	16	20	12	40
3	8	12	8	9	70
Demand	30	25	35	40	

Objective Question

1. Transportation problem is basically a
   (a) Maximization problem (b) minimization Problem
   (c) Optimization Problem (d) Traveling problem
2. To balance the transportation problem we have to introduce a dummy row or column in the matrix.
   (a) Key column (b) Key row
   (c) Dummy column (d) Slack row
3. To convert the transportation problem into a maximization model we have to:
   (a) Write the inverse of the matrix.
   (b) Multiply the rim requirements by -1.
   (c) To multiply the matrix by -1.
   (d) We cannot convert the transportation problem into a maximization problem .

4. In a transportation problem where the demand or requirement is equal to the available resources is known as:
(a) Balanced transportation problem
(b) Regular transportation problem
(c) Resource allocation transportation problem
(d) Simple transportation model

5. The total number of allocation in a basic feasible solution of transportation problem of m × n size is equal to:
(a) m × n (b) (m / n) -1
(c) (m + n + 1) (d) (m + n - 1)

6. When the total allocation in a transportation model of m × n size is not equal to (m+ n-1) the situation is known as:
(a) Unbalance situation (b) Tie situation
(c) Degeneracy (d) None of the above

7. The opportunity cost of a row in a transportation problem is obtained by:
(a) Deducting the smallest element in the row from all other elements of the row.
(b) Adding the smallest element in the row to all other elements of the row.
(c) Deducting the smallest element in the row from the next highest element of the row.
(d) Deducting the smallest element in the row from the highest element in that row.

8. In case the cost elements of one or two cells are not given in the problem, it means:
(a) The given problem is wrong
(b) We can allocate zeros to those cells.
(c) Allocate very high cost element to those cells.
(d) To assume that the route connected by those cells are not available.

9. To solve degeneracy in the transportation problem we have to:
(a) Put allocation in one of the empty cells as zero.

(b) Put a small element epsilon in any one of empty cells.
(c) Allocate the smallest element epsilon in such cell, which will not form a closed loop with other loaded cells.
(d) Allocate the smallest element epsilon in such a cell, which will form a closed loop with other loaded cells.

10. VAM stands for
    (a) Vogel's approximation Method
    (b) Vogel's Model
    (c) Value Added Method
    (d) Value approximation Method

11. MODI stands for
    (a) Modified method
    (b) Modified distribution method
    (c) Modified Delegation method
    (d) Most opportunity distribution method

[Ans. 1(b) 2 (c) 3 (c) 4 (a) 5 (d) 6 (c) 7 (c) 8 (d) 9 (c) 10 (a) 11(b)]

Chapter **6**

Assignment Problem

Course Outline

6.1 Introduction

Assignment Problem is a special case of Transportation problem and transportation problem is a special case of Linear Programming problem, therefore it is a special case of linear programming problem. The objective of the assignment problem is to assign a no. of tasks or jobs to an equal no. of persons or machine at a minimum cost or maximum profit. Basically assignment problem is a minimization problem.

For solving the assignment problem, we use assignment technique (Hungarian method). Since it is a special case of LPP thus it must have following properties.

1. An objective function
2. It must have constraints
3. It must have non negativity constraint
4. The relationship between variable and constraints must have linear.

6.2 Assignment Problem

There are four type of problem in assignment. They are:

1. Assigning the jobs to machine (persons) when the problem has square matrix i.e. the jobs are equals to the no. of machine (persons) to minimize the cost.
2. The second is maximization type of assignment problem. Here we have to assign certain jobs to certain facilities to maximize the returns.
3. Assignment problem having non-square matrix. Hence by adding a dummy row or dummy column for converting a non square matrix into square matrix to solve the problem.
4. Assignment problem with restrictions. Here restrictions such as a job cannot be done on a certain machine or a job cannot be allocated to a certain facility may be specified.
5. Traveling sales man problem (cycle type). Here a sales man must tour certain cities starting from his hometown and come back to his town after visiting all cities.

6.3 Comparison Between Transportation Problem & Assignment Problem:

Similarities:

Both are special case of LPP.

1. Both have objective function, constraints and non-negativity constraints. And the relationship between variables and constraints are linear.
2. Both are basically minimization problem.
3. The coefficients of variables are the solutions will be either zero or one in both the case.

Differences:

Transportation Problem	Assignment Problem
1. The matrix of the Problem may be Rectangular matrix or square matrix.	1. The matrix of the problem must be a Square matrix.
2. Depending on the condition of Problem the rows, columns may have any no. of allocations	2. Each rows and columns must have one to one allocation.
3. The basic feasible solution is obtained by NWC method, Least cost method or VAM.	3. The basic feasible solution is obtained by Hungarian method.
4. The optimality test is given by Stepping Stone method or by MODI method.	4. Optimality test is given by drawing Minimum no. of horizontal and vertical Lines to cover all zeros in the matrix.
5. The basic feasible solution must be **(m + n -1)** allocation.	5. Every column & row must have at least One zero.
6. The capacity & requirement value is the equal to a_i & b_j for the ith source & j^{th} Destinations. (i=1,2......m, j=1,2.........n)	6. For each source of each destination capacity and the require value is exactly One.
7. The problem is unbalanced if the total supply and total demand are not equal.	7. The Problem is unbalanced if the cost Matrix is not a square matrix.

6.4 Definitions and Mathematical formulation:

Assume that there are n jobs to be computed by n persons. Suppose each person can do each job at a time, with varying degree of efficiency. Let C_{ij} be the cost if the ith person is assigned to the jth job.

The problem is to assign one job to one person at a minimum cost.

The Assignment problem can be represented by n x n cost matrix $[C_{ij}]$ which is

	Persons					
		1	2	3………	j………	n
Persons	1	C_{11}	C_{12}	C_{13}………	C_{1j}………	C_{1n}
	2	C_{21}	C_{22}	C_{23}………	C_{2j}………	C_{2n}
	3					
	.					
	.					
	i	C_{i1}	C_{i2}	C_{i3}………	C_{ij}………	C_{in}
	.	.				
	.	.				
	n	C_{n1}	C_{n2}	C_{n3}………	C_{nj}………	C_{nn}

Mathematically the assignment problem can be represented as

$$\text{Minimise } (Z) = \sum_{i=1}^{n} \sum_{j=1}^{n} C_{ij} X_{ij} \qquad i=1,2\ldots\ldots n \quad j=1,2\ldots\ldots n$$

$$X_{ij} = \begin{cases} 1 & \text{if the } i^{th} \text{ person is assigned } j^{th} \text{job} \\ 0 & \text{if not} \end{cases}$$

Subject to the restrictions.

1. $\sum_{i=1}^{n} X_{ij} = 1, \ j=1,2\ldots\ldots n$

which means that only one job I done by the ith person, i=1,2….n

2. $\sum_{j=1}^{n} X_{ij} = 1, \ i=1,2\ldots\ldots n$

Which means that only one person should be assigned to the jth job, j=1,2……n

6.5 Hungarian Method

Hungarian method is a technique for solving the assignment problem.

STEP 1: Prepare a cost matrix. If the cost matrix is not a square matrix then add a dummy row (column) with zero cost elements.

STEP 2: 1) Deduct the smallest element in each row from the other elements of the respective rows.

2) Further modify the resulting matrix by deducting the smallest element of each column from all the element of the respective columns. Thus obtain the modify matrix.

STEP 3: Then draw the minimum no. of horizontal and vertical lines to cover all zero's is the resulting matrix. Let the minimum no. of lines be N. Now these are two possible cases. Case (i) If N=n, where are n is the order of matrix; then an optimal assignment can be made so make the assignment to get the required solution then go to step 6. Case (ii) If N<n then go to step 4.

STEP 4: Substrcting the smallest uncovered element from all uncovered elements and add the same element at the intersection of horizontal and vertical lines. Thus the modified matrix is obtained.

STEP 5: Repeat step 2 and 3 until we get the case (i) of step 3.

STEP 6: To make an assignment, examine the rows successively until a row-wise exactly single zero is found. Mark bracket ( ) on this zero to make the assignment **(0)**. Then mark a cross (X) over all zero if lying in the column of the square zero, showing that they can't be considered for future assignment. Continue this process until the entire zero has been examined. Repeat the same procedure for column also.

STEP 7: Repeat the step 6 successively until no unmarked zero is left in the matrix.

STEP 8: Thus exactly one marked squared zero in each row and each column of the matrix is obtained. The assignment corresponding to this marked bracket zero will give the optimal assignment.

6.6 Unbalance Assignment Problems

An assignment problem is called an unbalanced assignment

problem whenever the no. of tasks (jobs) is not equal to the no. of persons or machines. For the solution of such problems we have to add the dummy row or column to the given matrix to make it a square matrix.

6.7 Maximization Assignment Problems

When the assignment problem deals with the maximization of the objective function or we can say that the problem may be to assign persons to the jobs in such a manner that the expected profit is maximized. For solving this type of problem, we have to convert the maximization problem into minimization problem by the following two ways:

1) Subtract each element of the given matrix from the greatest element of the matrix to get the equivalent cost matrix.

OR

2) Place minus sign before each element of the project matrix to get the equivalent cost matrix.

6.8 Restrictions on Assignment Problem

Whenever we have to solve the assignment problem under some restrictions of a particular jobs to a particular person is not permitted then for overcoming this difficulty a very high cost (infinite cost) is assigned to the corresponding cell, which automatically exclude this activity from the optimal solution.

6.9 The Traveling Salesman Problem

Suppose a salesman has to visit n cities. We can start from any city, visit each city once and then return to his starting point. The objective is to select the sequence in which the cities are visited in such a way that his total traveling time is minimized.

The mathematical representation of the problem is

$$\text{Minimize } (Z) = \sum_{i=1}^{n} \sum_{j=1}^{n} C_{ij} \text{ for all } i \text{ and } j = 1, 2, \ldots\ldots\ldots\ldots n$$

Subject to the constraints.

$$\sum_{j=1}^{n} X_{ij} = 1, \quad i=2\ldots\ldots\ldots\ldots\ldots n$$

$$\sum_{i=1}^{n} X_{ij}=1, \quad j=2\ldots\ldots\ldots\ldots\ldots n$$

and all $X_{ij} \geq 0$ for all i and j

where C_{ij} be the distance or time or cost of going from city i to city j the decision variable X_{ij} be 1 if the salesman travels from city i to city j and otherwise 0.

In particular, going from i directly to i is not permitted which means $C_{ij} = \infty$ when i=j.

Example 1: Five jobs are to be assigned to five machines to minimize the total time required to process the job on machine. The time in hours for processing each job on each machine is given in the matrix below. By using assignment algorithm make the assignment for minimizing the time of processing.

Machines (Time in hours)

	V	W	X	Y	Z	
	A	2	4	3	5	4
	B	7	4	6	8	4
Jobs	C	2	9	8	10	4
	D	8	6	12	7	4
	E	2	8	5	8	8

Solution:

Step 1. Deduct the smallest element of each column from the corresponding column of the entire element in the matrix.

	V	W	X	Y	Z
A	0	0	0	0	0
B	5	0	3	3	0
C	0	5	5	5	0
D	6	2	9	2	0
E	0	4	2	3	4

Step 2. Since in each row at least one zeros, therefore the element of row will not change.

	V	W	X	Y	Z
A	0	0	0	0	0
B	5	0	3	3	0
C	0	5	5	5	0
D	6	2	9	2	0
E	0	4	2	3	4

Step 3. Draw the minimum number of lines, which cover all the zeros of the matrix.

	V	W	X	Y	Z
A	0	0	0	0	0
B	5	0	3	3	0
C	0	5	5	5	0
D	6	2	9	2	0
E	0	4	2	3	4

Number of lines drawn to cover zero is N= 4 which is less than of the order of the matrix (n = 5). Thus go to the next step.

Step 4. Now we find the modified matrix by subtracting the smallest uncovered element from all the uncovered element and add to the element that is the point of interaction of lines. After that draw the minimum number of lines, which covers all the zeros of the matrix.

	V	W	X	Y	Z
A	2	0	0	0	2
B	7	0	3	3	2
C	0	3	3	3	0
D	6	0	7	0	0
E	0	2	0	1	4

Since the Number of lines drawn to cover all zeros (N=5) is equal to the order of the matrix (n=5). Hence we can make an assignments in the above matrix.

Step 5:

	V	W	X	Y	Z
A	2	0 (×)	0 (×)	(0)	2
B	7	(0)	3	3	2
C	(0)	3	3	3	0 (×)
D	6	0 (×)	7	0 (×)	(0)
E	0 (×)	2	(0)	1	4

First solution:

Jobs	**Machines**	**Cost**
A	Y	5
B	W	4
C	V	2
D	Z	4
E	X	5
Total Cost		= 20 hrs

Or

	V	W	X	Y	Z
A	2	0 (×)	(0)	0 (×)	2
B	7	(0)	3	3	2
C	0 (×)	3	3	3	(0)
D	6	0 (×)	7	(0)	0 (×)
E	(0)	2	0 (×)	1	4

Second solution:

Jobs	Machines	Cost
A	X	3
B	W	4
C	Z	4
D	Y	7
E	V	2
Total Cost		= 20 hrs

Example 2: A company has 5 jobs to be done on five machines. Assign the jobs for different machines as to minimize the total cost.

	A	B	C	D	E
1	13	8	16	18	19
2	9	15	24	9	12
3	12	9	4	4	4
4	6	12	10	8	13
5	15	17	18	12	20

Solution:

Step 1. Deduct the smallest element of each row from the corresponding row of the entire element in the matrix. And also deduct the smallest element of each column from the corresponding column of the entire element in the matrix. Then the reduced matrix is

	A	B	C	D	E
1	5	0	8	10	11
2	0	6	15	0	3
3	8	5	0	0	0
4	0	6	4	2	7
5	3	5	6	0	8

Step 2. Draw the minimum number of lines, which cover all the zeros of the matrix.

	A	B	C	D	E
1	5	0	8	10	11
2	0	6	15	0	3
3	8	5	0	0	0
4	0	6	4	3	7
5	3	5	6	0	8

Number of lines drawn to cover zero is (N=4), less than the order of matrix (n=5).

Step 3. Now we find the second modified matrix by subtracting the smallest uncover element from the entire uncovered element and add to the element, which is in the point of interaction of lines. After that draw the minimum number of lines to cover all zeros of the matrix.

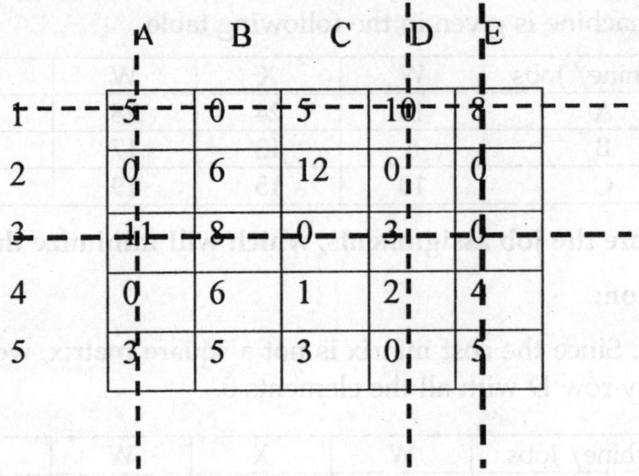

	A	B	C	D	E
1	5	0	5	10	8
2	0	6	12	0	0
3	11	8	0	3	0
4	0	6	1	2	4
5	3	5	3	0	5

Number of lines drawn to cover all zeros (N=5) is equal to the order of matrix.

Hence, we can make an assignment.

Step 5.

	A	B	C	D	E
1	5	(0)	5	10	8
2	0 (X)	6	12	0 (X)	(0)
3	11	8	(0)	3	0 (X)
4	(0)	6	1	2	4
5	3	5	3	(0)	5

Jobs	Machines	Cost
1	B	8
2	E	12
3	C	4
4	A	6
5	D	12
Total Cost		Rs. 42

Example of Unbalance Problem:

Example 3: A company has 4 machines to do 3 jobs. Each job can assign to one and only one machine. The cost of each job on each machine is given in the following table.

Machine/ Jobs	W	X	W	Z
A	18	24	28	32
B	8	13	17	19
C	10	15	19	22

What are the job assignments, which will minimize the cost?

Solution:

Step 1. Since the cost matrix is not a square matrix, we add a dummy row D with all the elements 0.

Machine/ Jobs	W	X	W	Z
A	18	24	28	32
B	8	13	17	18
C	10	15	19	22
D	0	0	0	0

Step 2. Subtract the minimum element in each row from all the elements in its row.

Machine/ Jobs	W	X	W	Z
A	0	6	10	14
B	0	5	9	11
C	0	5	9	12
D	0	0	0	0

Step 3. Each column has minimum element we draw minimum number of lines to cover all the zeros of the matrix.

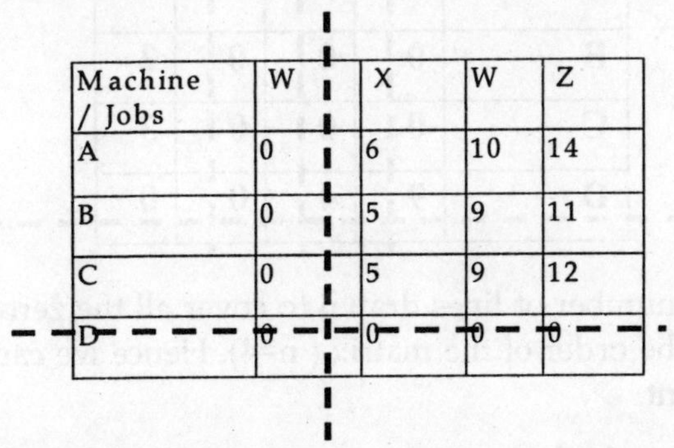

Machine / Jobs	W	X	W	Z
A	0	6	10	14
B	0	5	9	11
C	0	5	9	12
D	0	0	0	0

The number of lines drawn to cover all zeros (N=2) is less than the order of the matrix (n=4).

Step 4. Now we subtract the smallest uncover element from, all the uncovered elements and add to the element at the point of intersection. After that in the next modified matrix we draw minimum number of lines to cover all zeros of the matrix.

Machine / Jobs	**W**	**X**	**W**	**Z**
A	**0**	**1**	**5**	**9**
B	**0**	**0**	**4**	**6**
C	**0**	**0**	**4**	**7**
D	**5**	**0**	**0**	**0**

Since the number of lines drawn to cover all zeros (N=3) is less than the order of the matrix (n=4).Thus go to the next step.

Step 5. Again subtract the smallest uncover element from all, the uncovered elements and add to the element at the point of intersection.

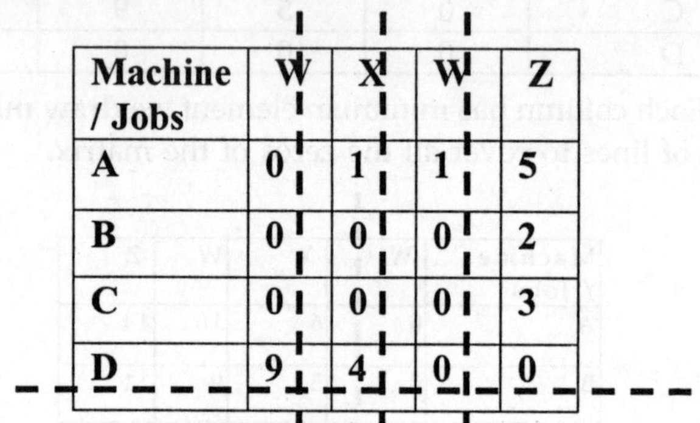

Machine / Jobs	W	X	W	Z
A	0	1	1	5
B	0	0	0	2
C	0	0	0	3
D	9	4	0	0

Here the number of lines drawn to cover all the zeros (N=4) is equal to the order of the matrix (n=4). Hence we can make an assignment.

Step.6 Assignment

Machine / Jobs	W	X	W	Z
A	(0)	1	1	4
B	0 (x)	(0)	0 (x)	1
C	0 (x)	0 (x)	(0)	3
D	9	4	0 (x)	(0)

Jobs	Machines
A	W
B	X
C	Y
D	Z

Or

(2)

Machine / Jobs	W	X	W	Z
A	(0)	1	1	4
B	0 (x)	0 (x)	(0)	1
C	0 (x)	(0)	0 (x)	3
D	9	4	0 (x)	(0)

Jobs	Machines
A	W
B	Y
C	X
D	Z

Example of Maximization Problem:

Example 4: a company has five jobs V, W, X, Y, Z and five machine A, B, C, D and E. The given matrix shows the returns in Rs. of assigning a job to a machine. Assign the job to machine so as to maximize the total returns.

Machines/Jobs	A	B	C	D	E
V	5	11	10	12	4
W	2	4	6	3	5
X	3	12	5	14	6
Y	6	14	4	11	7
Z	7	9	8	12	5

Solution: The objective is to maximize the total returns. We have to convert the given problem into minimization problem.

Step 1. Subtract all the element of the matrix from the highest element (14) of the matrix.

Machines/Jobs	A	B	C	D	E
V	9	3	4	2	10
W	12	10	8	11	9
X	11	2	9	0	8
Y	8	0	10	3	7
Z	7	5	6	2	9

Step 2. Deduct the smallest element of each row from the corresponding row of the entire element in the matrix.

Machines/Jobs	A	B	C	D	E
V	7	1	2	0	8
W	4	2	0	3	1
X	11	2	9	0	8
Y	8	0	10	3	7
Z	5	3	4	0	7

Step 3. Deduct the smallest element of each column from the corresponding column of the entire element in the matrix. Then the reduced matrix is:

Machines/Jobs	A	B	C	D	E
V	3	1	2	0	7
W	0	2	0	3	0
X	7	2	9	0	7
Y	4	0	10	3	6
Z	1	3	4	0	6

Step 4. Draw minimum numbers of lines cover all zeros of the above matrix.

Machines /Jobs	A	B	C	D	E
V	3	1	2	0	7
W	0	2	0	3	0
X	7	2	9	0	7
Y	4	0	10	3	6
Z	1	3	4	0	6

Since the number of lines drawn to cover all zeros (N=3) is less than the order of the matrix (n=5).Thus go to the next step.

Step 5. Now we subtract the smallest uncover element from all the uncovered elements and add to the element at the point of intersection. After that in the next modified matrix, we draw minimum number of lines to cover all zeros of the matrix.

Since the number of lines drawn to cover all zeros (N=4) is less than the order of the matrix (n=5). Thus go to the next step.

Machines /Jobs	A	B	C	D	E
V	2	0	1	0	6
W	0	2	0	4	0
X	5	1	8	0	6
Y	4	0	10	4	6
Z	0	2	3	0	5

Step 6. Again subtract the smallest uncover element from all, the uncovered elements and add to the element at the point of intersection and draw the minimum number of lines to cover all the zeros of the matrix.

Machines /Jobs	A	B	C	D	E
V	2	0	0	0	6
W	1	3	0	5	0
X	6	1	7	0	5
Y	4	0	10	4	5
Z	0	2	2	0	4

Here the number of lines drawn to cover all the zeros (N=5) of the matrix is equal to the order of the matrix (n=5). Hence we can make an assignment.

Step 7. Assignment

Machines /Jobs	A	B	C	D	E
V	2	0 (x)	(0)	1	6
W	1	3	0 (x)	6	(0)
X	5	0(x)	6	(0)	4
Y	4	(0)	10	5	5
Z	(0)	2	2	1	4

Jobs	Machines	Profit
V	C	10
W	E	5
X	D	14
Y	B	14
Z	A	7
Total maximum Profit =		Rs 50

Example of Restrictions Problem:

Example 5: Solve the following assignment problem:

Machines/ Jobs	I	II	III	IV	V
A	9	11	15	10	11
B	12	9	–	10	9
C	–	11	14	11	7
D	14	8	12	7	8

Solution. Step 1. According to the given matrix Job B can not be assigned to Machine IIIAnd Job C can not be assigned to machine I, so we assign a very high cost ∞ in the cells (B, III) and (C, I).

Machines/ Jobs	I	II	III	IV	V
A	9	11	15	10	11
B	12	9	∞	10	9
C	∞	11	14	11	7
D	14	8	12	7	8

Step 2. Above matrix is not a square matrix i.e it is a unbalance assignment problem so we add a dummy row (E) with zero cost in all cells of this row. Therefore we have:

Machines/ Jobs	I	II	III	IV	V
A	9	11	15	10	11
B	12	9	∞	10	9
C	∞	11	14	11	7
D	14	8	12	7	8
E	0	0	0	0	0

Step 3. Deduct the smallest element of each column from the corresponding column of the entire element in the matrix. Then the reduced matrix is:

Machines/ Jobs	I	II	III	IV	V
A	0	2	6	1	2
B	3	0	∞	1	0
C	∞	4	7	4	0
D	7	1	5	0	1
E	0	0	0	0	0

Step 4. Each column has minimum element we draw minimum number of lines to covers all the zeros of the matrix.

Machines/ Jobs	I	II	III	IV	V
A	0	2	6	1	2
B	3	0	∞	1	0
C	∞	4	7	4	0
D	7	1	5	0	1
E	0	0	0	0	0

Step 5. Here the number of lines drawn to cover all the zeros (N=5) of the matrix is equal to the order of the matrix (n=5). Hence we can make an assignment.

Machines/ Jobs	I	II	III	IV	V
A	(0)	2	6	1	2
B	3	(0)	∞	1	0(x)
C	∞	4	7	4	(0)
D	7	1	5	(0)	1
E	0(x)	0(x)	(0)	0(x)	0(x)

Since there is an assignment in each row and column, so the optimal assignment is:

Jobs	Machines	Cost
A	I	9
B	II	9
C	V	7
D	IV	7
Total minimum cost	=	Rs 32

Example of Traveling salesman problem:

Example 6: A traveling salesman has to visit 5 cities. He wishes to start from a particular city, visit each city one and then return to his starting point. Cost of going from one city to another is shown below. Find the least cost route.

	A	B	C	D	E
A	∞	16	18	13	20
B	21	∞	16	27	14
C	12	14	∞	15	21
D	11	18	19	∞	21
E	16	14	17	12	∞

Solution: Step 1. Deduct the smallest element of each row from the corresponding row of the entire element in the matrix.

	A	B	C	D	E
A	∞	3	5	0	7
B	7	∞	2	13	0
C	0	2	∞	3	9
D	0	7	8	∞	10
E	4	2	5	0	∞

Step 2. Deduct the smallest element of each column from the corresponding column of the entire element in the matrix. Then the reduced matrix is:

	A	B	C	D	E
A	∞	1	3	0	7
B	7	∞	0	13	0
C	0	0	∞	3	9
D	0	5	6	∞	10
E	4	0	3	0	∞

Step 3. Draw minimum number of lines to covers all the zeros of the matrix.

	A	B	C	D	E
A	∞	1	3	0	7
B	7	∞	0	13	0
C	0	0	∞	3	9
D	0	5	6	∞	10
E	4	0	3	0	∞

Since the number of lines drawn to cover all zeros (N=4) is less than the order of the matrix (n=5). Thus go to the next step.

Step 4. Now we subtract the smallest uncover element from, all the uncovered elements and add to the element at the point of intersection. After that in the next modified matrix, we draw minimum number of lines to cover all zeros of the matrix.

	A	B	C	D	E
A	∞	1	0	0	4
B	10	∞	0	16	0
C	0	0	∞	3	6
D	0	5	3	∞	7
E	4	0	0	0	∞

Step 6. Here the number of lines drawn to cover all the zeros (N=5) of the matrix is equal to the order of the matrix (n=5). Hence we can make an assignment.

	A	B	C	D	E
A	∞	1	(0)	0(x)	4
B	10	∞	0(x)	16	(0)
C	0(x)	(0)	∞	3	6
D	(0)	5	3	∞	7
E	4	0(x)	0(x)	(0)	∞

The salesman can follow the following path:

City	to	City	Distance
A	to	C	18
C	to	B	14
B	to	E	14
E	to	D	12
D	to	A	11
The total distance travel by the sales man		=	**69 km**

(ii)

	A	B	C	D	E
A	∞	1	0(x)	(0)	4
B	10	∞	0(x)	16	(0)
C	0(x)	(0)	∞	3	6
D	(0)	5	3	∞	7
E	4	0(x)	(0)	0(x)	∞

City	City
A	D
B	E
C	B
D	A
E	C

As the salesman should go from A to d and come back to A without covering B, C, E which is contradicting the fact that no city is twice before all the cities are visited.

6.10 Practice Problem:

1. Define the assignment problem with the help of an example.
2. Give the mathematical formulation of the assignment problem.
3. Write the short notes on following.
   (a) Hungarian Method
   (b) Unbalance Assignment Problem
   (c) Maximization case in assignment problem
   (d) Traveling salesman problem
   (e) Restriction in assignment problem
4. Explain the difference between Assignment Problem and Transportation Problem.
5. Describe the algorithm for solving the assignment Problem.
6. Solve the following Assignment Problem:

(a)

	A	B	C	D
I	1	4	6	3
II	9	7	10	9
III	4	5	11	7
IV	8	7	8	5

(b)

	A	B	C	D
I	10	25	15	20
II	15	30	5	15
III	35	20	12	24
IV	17	25	24	20

7. A machine operator processes five types of items on his machine each week and must choose a sequence for them. The setup cost per change depends on the items presently on the machine and the set-up to be made according to the following table:

	A	B	C	D	E
A	∞	4	7	3	4
B	4	∞	6	3	4
C	7	6	∞	7	5
D	3	3	7	∞	7
E	4	4	5	7	∞

If he process each type of items once only once in each week, how should he sequence the items on his machine in order to minimize the total set-up cost?

8. A marketing manager has five salesman and there are 5 sales districts. Considering the capabilities of the salesman and the nature of district, the estimates made by the marketing manager for the sales per month (in 1000 rupees)for each salesman in each district would be as follows:

	A	B	C	D	E
1	32	38	40	28	40
2	40	24	28	21	36
3	41	27	33	30	37
4	22	38	41	36	36
5	29	33	40	35	3

Find the assignment of salesman to the districts that will result in the maximum sales.

9. A company is faced with the problem of assigning 4 machines to 6 different jobs (one machine to one job only) . The profits are estimated as follows:

	A	B	C	D
1	3	6	2	6
2	7	1	4	4
3	3	8	5	8
4	6	4	3	7
5	5	2	4	3
6	5	7	6	4

10. Four different job can be done on four different machine and take down time costs are prohibitively high for change over. The matrix below gives the cost in rupees of producing jobs i on machine j.

Jobs	Machines			
	M_1	M_2	M_3	M_4
J_1	5	7	11	6
J_2	8	5	9	6
J_3	4	7	10	7
J_4	10	4	8	3

Objective Question:

1. Assignment problem is basically a
   (a) Maximization Problem
   (b) Minimization Problem
   (C) Transportation Problem
   (d) Primal Problem
2. The assignment Problem is Solved by
   (a) Simplex Method
   (b) Graphical method
   (c) Vector Method
   (d) Hungarian Method
3. In Hungarian method of solving assignment problem, the row opportunity cost matrix is obtained by:
   (a) Dividing each row by the elements of the row above.
   (b) Subtracting the element of the row from the elements of the row above it.
   (c) Subtracting the smallest element from all other elements of the row.
   (d) Subtracting all the elements of the row from the highest element in the matrix.
4. The horizontal and vertical lines drawn to cover all zeros of the matrix must be:
   (a) equal to each other
   (b) Equal to m × n
   (c) Equal to m+n
   (d) Number of rows or column.

5. The assignment matrix is always
   (a) Rectangular Matrix
   (b) Square Matrix
   (c) Identity Matrix
   (d) None of the above

6. To balance an assignment matrix we have to
   (a) Open a dummy row
   (b) Open a dummy column
   (c) Open either a dummy row or column depending upon the situation.
   (d) We can not balance the assignment problem.

7. To covert the assignment problem in to maximization problem:
   (a) Deduct the smallest element in the matrix from all other element of the row.
   (b) All elements of the matrix are deducted from the highest element in the matrix.
   (c) Deduct smallest element in any row from all other elements of the row.
   (d) Deduct all elements of the row from highest element in that row.

8. The similarity between Assignment and Transportation problem is :
   (a) Both are rectangular matrix.
   (b) Both are square matrix.
   (c) Both can be solved by graphical method.
   (d) Both have objective function and non-negativity constraints.

9. The assignment problem will have an alternate solutions:
   (a) When total opportunity cost matrix has at least one zero in each row and column.
   (b) When all rows have two zeros.

   (c) When there is a tie between zero opportunity cost cells.
   (d) If two diagonal elements are zeros.

10. The following character dictates that assignment matrix is a square matrix:
   (a) The allocation in assignment problem is one to one.
   (b) Because we find row opportunity cost matrix.
   (c) Because we find column opportunity cost matrix.
   (d) Because make allocations , one has to draw horizontal and vertical lines.

(Ans. 1 (b), 2 (d), 3 (c), 4 (c), 5 (b), 6 (c), 7 (b), 8 (d), 9 (b), 10 (a)

Chapter **7**

Sequencing Problem

Course Outline

7.1 Introduction

In the sequencing problem, we have to determine the order or sequence in which the jobs are to be processed through machines so as to minimize the total processing time.

There are the problems in which we have n tasks to be processed on same or all of m different machines in which the total effectiveness depends on the order of processing.

There are $[(n!)^m]$ possible sequence for the problem. It is very difficult to select the most suitable sequence from a large number of sequence $[(n!)^m]$ which optimizes the total effectiveness so this chapter deals with sequencing problems. The sequencing problem is basically a minimization problem.

7.2 Definition (A sequencing Problem)

A general sequencing problem may be defined as follows:

Let there be 'n' jobs (J_1, J_2, J_3.........J_n), which are to be processed on 'm' machines ($M_1 M_2, M_3$,.........M_n). The order of the machines for each job in which it should go to the machine is given. The time is required by the jobs on each of the machines is also given. Then the problem is to find the sequence which minimize the total time or cost.

7.3 General Assumptions

1. The processing times for each job are exactly known and independent of there processing order.
2. Each job, once started on the machine, we should not stop the processing in the middle.
3. No machine may process more than one job at a time.
4. The time taken by the jobs in going from one machine to another is negligible.
5. There is exactly one machine of each type.
6. A job is processed as soon as possible in sequencing order.
7. All jobs are known and are ready to start processing.

7.4 Types of sequencing Problem

There are generally four types of sequencing problem.

(a) Sequencing problem for n-jobs on two machines.

(b) Sequencing problem for n-jobs on three machines.

(c) Sequencing problem for n-jobs on m-machines.

(d) Sequencing problem for two jobs on m-machines.

7.5 Solutions for sequencing problems

(a) Sequencing Problem for n-jobs on two machines:

Johnson's Method

Let us consider the problem of processing n-jobs (J_1, J_2, J_3.........J_n) on two machines and under the following assumption.

1. Each job is processed in the order AB.
2. A_i = Processing time of ith job on machine A.(i=1,2,3.......n)
3. B_i= Processing time of ith job on machine B.(i=1,2,3........n)

The objective is to find the sequence of jobs so as to minimize the total elapsed time (T) with the help of following table.

Machines/ Job	1	2	3	....n
A	A_1	A_2	A_3	....A_n
B	B_1	B_2	B_3	....B_n

The Johnson's and Bellman procedure for determining an optimal sequence is as follows.

Step 1. Select the smallest processing time in the lists $A_1, A_2, \ldots A_n$ and $B_1, B_2, \ldots B_n$. Suppose minimum processing time occur for job **k**.

Step 2. If the smallest processing time is for machine A. Thus the kth job process first and place it in the beginning of sequence. If it is for the machine B process the kth job in the last and place it at the end of the sequence.

Step 3. If there is a tie in selecting the minimum processing time then there may be four cases.

Case 1. If the equal minimum value occurs for the machine **A**, select the job with larger processing time in **B** for placing in the job sequence first.

Case 2. If the equal minimum values occur only for the machine **B** select the job with larger processing time in **A** to be sequenced in the job sequence last.

Case 3. If there are equal minimum values one for each machine then place the job in the machine **A** first and the one in the machine **B** last.

Case 4. If more number of jobs has the same minimum element in the same column, then the problem will have many alternate solutions.

Step 4. Delete the jobs already sequenced. If all jobs have been sequenced go to next step.

Step 5. Calculate the total elapsed time and Idle time for both the machines by using the following formula.

Idle time on A= (Time when the last job in the optimal sequenced is completed on machine B)-(Time when the last job in the optimal sequence is completed on machine A).

Idle Time on B= (When the first job in the optimal sequence starts on machine B)

$$+ \sum_{k=2}^{n} [\text{Time } k^{th} \text{ starts on machine B} - \text{time } (k-1)^{th} \text{ job finished on machine B}]$$

Total Elapsed Time = The time between starting the first job in the optimal sequence on machine A and completing the last job in the optimal sequence on machine B.

Example: There are six jobs each of which go through the two machines A and B in the order AB. Processing times are given below.

Machine/Job	1	2	3	4	5	6
A	5	9	4	7	8	6
B	7	4	8	3	9	5

Solutions:

The ordering of the jobs by using the Johnson's method from the above table is given below.

Step 1.

					4

Step 2.

3					4

Step 3.

3				2	4

Step 4.

3	1	5	6	2	4

Calculation of total elapsed time:

Job	A		B		Idle time of machine A	Idle time of machine B
	in time	out time	in time	out time		
3	0	4	4	12		4
1	4	9	12	19		0
5	9	17	19	28	=42-	0
6	17	23	28	33	39=3hrs	0
2	23	32	33	37		0
4	32	39	39	42*		2
				Total	3hrs	6hrs
Total Elapsed Time=42 hrs						

Example. Find the sequence that minimizes the total elapsed time required to complete the following table on two machines.

Machines /jobs	A	B	C	D	E	F	G	H	I
M_1	2	5	4	9	6	8	7	5	4
M_2	6	8	7	4	3	9	3	8	11

Solution:

In the above question, there is the tie between more than two jobs then problem will have alternate solution.

Step 1.

A								

Step 2.

A							E	G

Step 3.

A						D	E	G

Step 4.

A	I	C				D	E	G

Step 5.

A	I	C	B	H	F	D	E	G

Calculation of Total elapsed Time of the Jobs.

Job	Machine M_1		MachineM_2		Idle time of Machine M_1	Idle time of MachineM_2
	in time	out time	in time	out time		
A	0	2	2	8		2
I	2	6	8	19		0
C	6	10	19	26		0
B	10	15	26	34		0
H	15	20	34	42	=61-	0
F	20	28	42	51	50=11hrs	0
D	28	37	51	55		0
E	37	43	55	58		0
G	43	50	58	61*		0
				Total	**11hrs**	**2hrs**
Total Elapsed Time = 61hrs						

(b) Sequencing Problem for n-jobs on three machines

Modified Johnson's Method:

Let us consider the problem of processing n-jobs $J_1, J_2, J_3 \ldots\ldots\ldots J_n$ on three machines A, B, C under the following assumptions:

1. Each job is performed in the order ABC.
2. A_i= Processing time of ith job on machine A, i= 1,2,3…n.
3. B_i= Processing time of ith job on machine B, i=1,2,3….n.
4. C_i= processing time of ith job on machine C, I=1,2,3….n.

The objective is to find the sequence of jobs so as to minimizes the total elapsed time (T) with the help of following table:

Machine/ Jobs	1	2	3	……………n
A	A_1	A_2	A3	……………An
B	B_1	B_2	B_3	……………Bn
C	C_1	C_2	C_3	……………C_n

This method is applicable if any one of the condition is true.

(1) The smallest processing time for machine A^3. The largest processing time for machine B.

(2) The smallest processing time for machine C^3. The largest processing time for machine B.

The method is to replace the problem with an equivalent problem involving n-jobs on two machines. Suppose G and H denote the two machines then the processing time be G_i and H_i of ith [i =1,2,....n] job on these two machines are given by

$$G_i = A_i + B_i$$

and

$$H_i = B_i + C_i$$

Now find the optimal sequence of jobs in the order GH on these machines by using Johnson methods.

Example. We have five jobs, each of which must go through the machines A, B and C in the order ABC.

Machine/Job	**1**	**2**	**3**	**4**	**5**
A	5	7	6	9	5
B	2	1	4	5	3
C	3	7	5	6	7

Solution. Here

Minimum of A = 5

Maximum of B = 5

Minimum of C = 5

Since Minimum of A ≥ maximum of B

Then we have to convert three machines into two artificial machines. The processing of times of these two machines are given below:

Job	**Processing Time**	
	$G_i=A_i+B_i$	$H_i=B_i+C_i$
1	7	5
2	8	8
3	10	9
4	14	11
5	8	10

The order of the jobs are described in the following step.

Step 1.

5	2	4	3	1

Step 2.

2	5	4	3	1

Step 3.

5	4	3	2	1

Calculation of Elapsed time

Job	Machine A		Machine B		Machine C		Idle time of A	Idle time of B	Idle time of C
	In time	Out time	In time	Out time	In time	Out time			
2	0	7	7	8	8	15	=40-32 =8	7	8
5	7	12	12	15	15	22		4	-
4	12	21	21	26	26	32		6	4
3	21	27	27	31	32	37		1	-
1	27	32	32	34	37	40*		1+6	-
Total							8hrs	25hrs	12h rs

(c) Sequencing problem for n-Jobs on k-machines

Consider n jobs (1,2.....n) processing through k-machines (M_1, M_2,......M_k..) in the same order.

Step 1. Find Min. M_i and Min. M_k and Maximum of each of M_{i2}, M_{i3},.....M_{ik-1} for i=1,2,3...n

Step 2. Check the following:

Min M_{i1} ³ Max M_{ij}, for j= 2,3,....k-1 **or**
i i

Min M_{ik} ³ Max M_{ij}, for j=2,3.....k-1
i i

Step 3. If the inequality in step 2 is not satisfied the method otherwise go to next step.

Step 4. In addition to step 2 if $M_{i2}+M_{i3}+......M_{ik-1}=C$ where C is fixed constant for all i=1,2...n. Then determine the optimal sequence for n-jobs and the two machines are M_1 and M_k by using the Johnsons rule.

Step 5. If the condition $M_{i2}+M_{i3}+........M_{ik-1}{}^{1}$ C for all i =1,2....n, we define two machine G and H such that

$G_i = M_{i1}+M_{i2}+........+M_{ik-1.}$

$H_i = M_{i2}+M_{i3}+........+M_{ik}$ i=1,2,3......n.

Example. Find the total minimum elapsed time with the help of following table. If no passing of jobs is permitted.

Machines	Jobs			
	1	2	3	4
A	7	6	5	8
B	5	6	4	3
C	2	4	5	3
D	3	5	6	2
E	9	10	8	6

Solution: Since the problem is to be sequenced on five machines, we convert the problem into two machine problem by adopting the following steps.

Step 1. Find Min $(A_i, E_i) = (5,6)$ i=1,2,3,4

Max $(B_i, C_i, D_i) = (6,5,6)$

Step 2. The inequality

Min $E_i=6\ ^{3}$ Max (B_i, C_i, D_i) is satisfied. Therefore, we can convert the problem into two-machine problem.

Step 3. since $B_i+C_i+D_i{}^{1}$ C where C is a fixed constant, we define two machine G and H such that

$G_i = A_i+B_i+C_i+D_i$

$H_i = B_i+C_i+D_i+E_i$ i=1,2,3,4.

The order of the job is

1	3	2	4

Calculation of total elapsed time

Job	A		B		C		D		E		Idle time of A	Idle time of B	Idle time of C	Idle time of D	Idle tim e of E
	in	ou t	in	out	in	out	in	out	in	out					
1	0	7	7	12	12	14	14	17	17	26		7	12	14	17
3	7	12	12	16	16	21	21	27	27	35		0	2	4	1
2	12	18	18	24	24	28	28	33	35	45	=51-	2	3	1	0
4	18	26	26	29	29	32	33	35	45	51*	26=25	2+22	1+19	0+16	0
											25hrs	33hrs	37hrs	35hrs	18hr s

The total elapsed time =51 hrs

(d) Sequencing Problem of 2-jobs on 'M', machines

This type of problem can be solved with the help of graphical method.

Graphical Method

This method is applicable to solve the problems involving 2 jobs on 'm' machines.

Step 1. Represent Job 1 on X-axis and job 2 on Y-axis.

Step 2. The horizontal line on the graph shows the processing time of Job 1 and idle time of Job 2. Similarly a vertical line on the graph shows processing time of job 2 and idle time of job 1.

Step 3. Draw horizontal and vertical lines from points on X-axis and Y-axis to construct the blocks and hatch the blocks.

Step 4. Our job is to find the minimum time required to finish both the jobs in the given order of matching. Hence we have to follow inclined path, preferably a line include at 45 degrees.

Step 5. While drawing the include line, care must be taken to see that it will not pass through the region indication the matching of order job.

Step 6. After drawing the line, the total time taken is equals to time required for processing plus idle time for both job.

Note. The sum of processing time + idle time for both jobs must be same.

Example. 1 Use the graphical method to minimize the time needed to process the following jobs on two machine as shown

Job. 1		Job 2	
Sequence of machine	Time	Sequence of machine	Time
A	3	B	5
B	4	C	4
C	2	A	3
D	6	D	2
E	2	E	6

Also calculate

(i) For each machine find which should be done first.

(ii) Calculate total time needed to complete both the job.

Solution:

We draw the graph of the proble in the manner describe in article 15.8 as follows:

1. We draw lines (horizontal and vertical) 0X and 0Y representing the processing time of job 1 and 2 respectively.
2. Then we mark the processing time of the jobs on the machine in the given order as shown in figure.
3. Then we draw shaded rectangular blocks corresponding to each machine as shown in figure.
4. Now starting from the starting point O we ve on doing jobs avoiding the shaded rectangular blocks until the finished point is reached. Here it is important to note that we shall try to move as much as we can along a line at angle 45° to the horizontal wherever movement along this line is not possible we shall move only horizontally or

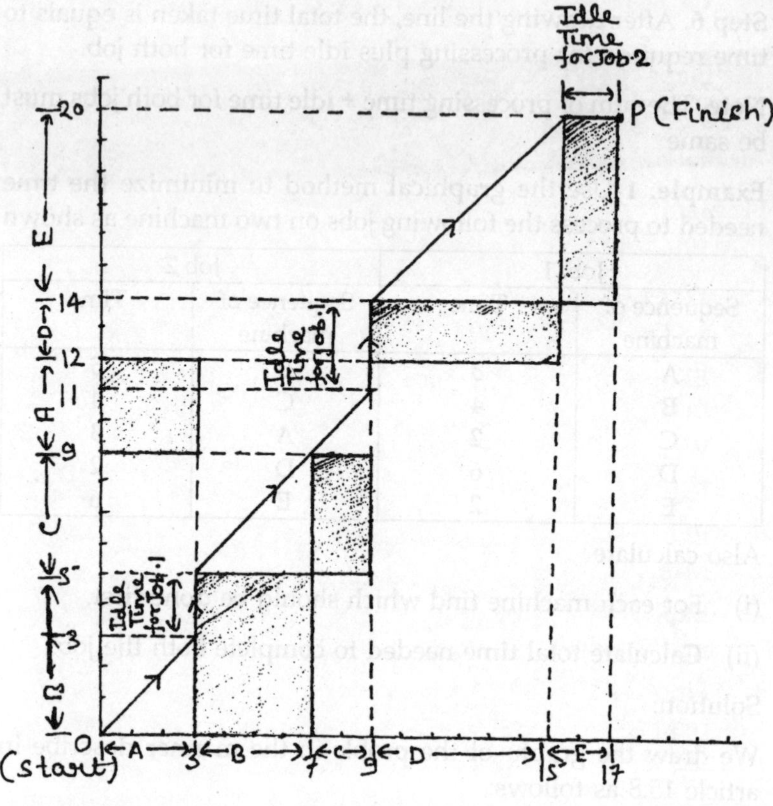

vertically (as needed).

The best path shown in figure by arrows.

It is clear from the graph that we have processed.

Job 1 before Job 2 on Machine A

Job 2 before Job 1 on Machine B

Job 2 before Job 1 on Machine C

Job 2 before Job 1 on Machine D

Job 2 before Job 1 on Machine E

The Elapsed Time = Processing time of Job 1 + Idle time of job 1 = 17 + (2+3) = 22 Hours.

or

The Elapsed Time = Processing time of Job 2 + Idle time of Job 2 = 20 +2 = 22 Hours

7.6 Practice Problem

Problem

1. What is sequencing Problem?
2. Write down the general assumption regarding the sequential problem.
3. Explain the method of processing n-jobs through 2 – machines.
4. Write down the types of sequencing problem?
5. Explain how to process n- jobs through m-machines.
6. Explain the graphical method to solve two jobs through M-machines.
7. Explain the method of processing m-jobs through three machines A, B, and C in the order ABC.
8. Find the sequence that minimizes the total elapsed time required to complete the following tasks.

Job	1	2	3	4	5	6
Machine.I	5	9	4	7	8	6
Machine.II	7	4	8	3	9	5

9. There are seven jobs each of which has to go through the machine M1 and M2 in the order $M_1.M_2$.Processing time (in hour) are given as.

Job	1	2	3	4	5	6	7
Machine.M_1	3	12	15	6	10	11	9
Machine.M_2	8	10	10	6	12	1	3

10. Find the sequence that minimizes the total elapsed time required to complete the following tasks.

Job	A	B	C	D	E	F	G
Machine.I	3	8	7	4	9	8	7
Machine.II	4	3	2	5	1	4	3
Machine.III	6	7	5	11	5	6	12

11. Find the sequence that minimizes the total elapsed time required to complete the following tasks.

	Machine			
	A	B	C	D
Job1	4	6	7	3
Job 2	4	7	5	8

Use graphical method to obtain the minimum elapsed time.

12. When passing is not allowed solve the following problem giving an optimal solution.

		Machine				
		M1	M2	M3	M4	M5
	A	9	7	4	5	11
Jobs	B	8	8	6	7	12
	C	7	6	7	8	10
	D	10	5	5	4	8

Objective Questions

1. The Objective of Sequencing problem is:
   a. To find the order in which jobs are to be made
   b. To find the time required for completing all the jobs on hand
   c. To find the sequence in which jobs on hand are to be processed to minimize the total time required for processing the jobs
   d. To maximize the effectiveness
2. The time required for printing of four books A, B, C & D is 5, 8, 10 & 7hrs. While its data entry requires 7, 4, 3, & 6 hrs respectively, the sequence time that minimizes total elapsed time is:
   a. ACBD
   b. ABCD
   c. ADCB
   d. CBDA

3. If there are 'n' jobs and 'm' machines, there will be .... sequences of doing the jobs.
   a. n×m
   b. m×n
   c. n^m
   d. $(n!)^m$
4. In general, sequence problem will be solved by using..............
   a. Hungarian Method
   b. Simplex Method
   c. Johnson & Bellman Method
   d. Flood's Technique
5. This is not allowed in sequencing of 'n' jobs on two machines
   a. Passing
   b. Loading
   c. Repeating the job
   d. Once loaded on the machine it should be completed before removing from the machine
6. Johnson Bellman rule states that
   a. If the smallest processing time occurs under the first machine, do that job first.
   b. If the smallest processing time occurs under the second machine, do that job first.
   c. If the smallest processing time occurs under the first machine, do that job last.
   d. If the smallest processing time occurs under the second machine keep the processing pending.
7. To convert 'n' jobs and 3-machine problem into 'n' jobs and 2-machine problem, the following rule must be satisfied
   a. All the processing times of second machine must be same
   b. The maximum processing time of 2nd machine must be = the minimum processing times of first and third machines

c. The maximum processing time of 1st machine must be = the minimum processing times of other two machines
d. The minimum processing time of 2nd machine must be = the minimum processing times of first and third machines

8. If jobs A & B have same processing times under Machine I and Machine II, then prefer
   a. Job A
   b. Job B
   c. Both A & B
   d. Either A or B
9. If a job is having minimum processing time under both the machines, Then the job is placed in:
   a. Any One (first or last) position
   b. Available last position
   c. Available first position
   d. Both first and last positions
10. The functional assumption of Johnson's method of sequencing is:
   a. No passing rule
   b. Passing rule
   c. Same type of machines are to be used
   d. Non zero process time
11. In a 2 jobs and 'n' machines problem a lie at 45° represents
   a. Job 2 is idle
   b. Job 1 is idle
   c. Both jobs are idle
   d. Both jobs are under processing

Answers:

1 (c), 2 (d), 3 (d), 4.(c), 5 (a), 6 (a), 7(b), 8.(d), 9 (a), 10 (b), 11 (d)

Chapter 8

Game Theory

Course outline

8.1 Introduction

Life is full of struggle and competitions. In many Practical problems, it is required to take decision in a situation where there are two or more opposite parties with conflicting interests and the action of one depends upon the action which the opponent takes. Such a situation is termed as a competitive situation.

The theory of Games is a mathematical theory that deals with the general features of competitive situations. This theory is helpful when 2 or more individual or organization with conflicting objective try to make decisions. In such a situation a decision made by one decision maker affects the decision made by one or more of the remaining decision makers and the final outcome depend upon the decision of all the parties. Such situations often arise in the fields of business, industry, economics, sociology and military training.

The theory of Games was developed by **John Von Neumann** in **1928**. After that he and **Morgenstern** have Mathematically dealt that theory and published a well known paper **"Theory**

of Games and Economic Behaviors" in 1944.

8.2 Definition

(Game Theory)

A competitive situation is called a Game. The termed Game represents a conflict between 2 or more parties. When we hear the word Game, we get to our mind like the pleasure giving games like Football, Badminton, Chess etc. In these Games we have 2 parties or group playing the game with definite well defined rules and regulations. The outcome of the game as decided to win any one party. In our discussion in Theory of Games, we are not concerned with pleasure giving Games but we are concerned with business games. Business games are related to company or industry for example firm struggling to maintain their market shares, launching advertisement campaigns by companies, marketing of competing product, negotiations between organizations and unions etc.

8.3 Type of Games

There are four type of Games:

1. **Two person Games**: A game with only 2 players in which the players may have many possible choices open to them for each play of the game. Hence, it is called two person game.
2. **n- person Game**: If the no. of players in the game is more than two, then the game is called n person game.
3. **zero sum game:** A Game is said to be a zero sum game if the sum of payments of all competitors is zero for every possible outcome of the game or if the sum of points won equals to the sum of the points lost.
4. **Two person zero sum game (Rectangular Game):** A Game with two players where the game of one player equals to the loss of another player is known as a two person zero sum game, it is also called rectangular game because their payoff matrix is in rectangular form.

8.4 Basic term used in Game Theory

1. Strategy
2. Payoff Matrix
3. The Maximin-Minimax principle
4. Saddle point

1. Strategy: The strategy of player is the predetermined rule by which a player decides his course of action from his own list of courses of action during the game. There are following two types of strategy:

(i) Pure Strategy: A pure strategy is a decision in advance of all plays, always to choose a particular course of action.

(ii) Mixed Strategy: A mix strategy is a decision in advance of all plays, to choose a course of action for each play in accordance with some particular Probability Distribution. Mixed Strategy is denoted by the set $S = \{x_1, x_2 .... x_n\}$

Where x_i is the probability of choosing the course "i" such that $x_i \geq 0$,

i=1, 2.......n &

$X_1+X_2+X_3+..................X_n=1$

$$\sum_{i=1}^{n} X_i = 1$$

2. Pay- Off Matrix: Pay off is the outcome of playing the game. A payoff matrix is a table which shows how payments should be made at the end of a play or game.

Let us consider a player A has m course of action & player B has n course of action then a payoff matrix may be constructed by using the following steps:

a) Each row of the matrix represents the course of action available to A.

b) Each column of the matrix represents the course of action available to B.

c) The cell entries are the payments to A for the one matrix and to B for the other Matrix . The cell entry a_{ij} is the payment to A in A's payoff matrix when A chooses the course of action i & B chooses the course of action j.

d) In the zero sum two person game, the cell entry in B's payoff matrix will be the negative of the corresponding cell entry in A's payoff matrix.

(A's pay off matrix)

		1	2	........i........	...n
	1	a_{11}	a_{12}........	a_{1j}........	a_{1n}
	2.	a_{21}	a_{22}........	a_{2j}........	a_{2n}.
A	i	a_{i1}	a_{i2}........	a_{ij}........	a_{in}
		a_{m1}	a_{m2}........	a_{mj}........	a_{mn}
	m				

3. The Maximini-Minimax Principles:

This principle is used for the selection of original strategies by two players. Consider two player **A** and **B**. **A** is a player who wishes to **maximize** his **gain** while player **B** wishes to **minimize** his **losses**. Since A would like to maximize his minimum gain, the value is called **Maximini Value** and the corresponding strategy is called the **Maximini strategy.**

On the other hand, since player B wishes to minimize his losses, the value is called Minimax value and the corresponding strategy is called **Minimax strategy.**

When these two are equals (Maximini Value = Minimax Value) the corresponding strategy is called 'optimal strategy' and the game is said to have a saddle point.

4. Saddle point:

A saddle point is a position in the payoff matrix where the maximum of row minima coincides with the minimum of column maxima. The payoff of the saddle point is called the **'Value of the Game'**.

Let us suppose that the maximini value is to be denoted by a and the minimax value is to be denoted by b and the value of the game by c.

Case 1.

A game is said to be fair if "Maximum value = Minimax Value = 0"

i.e. a= b=0

Case 2.

A game is said to be strictly determinable if " Maximini Value = Minimax value≠0"

i.e. a=b=c

8.5 Game Models

There are various types of Game models. They are based on the factor like the number of players, the sum of gains or losses and the number of strategies etc.

1. **Number of persons:** If the number of players is only two, it is called two–person game. If there are more than two players, it is called n-person game.
2. **Sum of pay-offs:** If the sum of gains and losses to the player is zero, the gain is called zero sum game otherwise non-zero sum game.
3. **Number of strategies:** If the number of strategies is finite, the game is called finite game otherwise it is called infinite game.

8.6 Characteristics of Games

A competitive game has following characteristics:

1. In a competitive game there must be finite number of participants.
2. Each participant has available to him a list of finite number

of course of action.

3. Each participant knows all the possible choices available to others but does not know which of them is going to be chosen by them.
4. A play is said to occur when each of the participants chooses one of the course of action available to him.
5. The outcome of the game is affected by the choices made by all the players.
6. The payoffs for each and every play are fixed and specified in advance and are known to each player.
7. Each outcome determines a set of payments **(+ ive, -ive or zero)** one to each competitor.

8.7 Rules of Game Theory:

(A) For Pure strategy:

(i) Two-person zero-sum Game with saddle point

This type of game can be solved with the help of Maximin-Minimax principles.

Example: The payoff matrix of game is given below. Find the solution of the game of A and B.

Solution:

	I	II	III	IV	V	Row Minimum
I	-2	0	0	5	3	-2
II	3	2	1	2	2	1
III	4	-3	0	-2	6	-4
IV	5	3	-4	2	-6	-6
Column Maximum	5	3	1	5	6	

Now Row Minimum = { -2, 1, -4,-6 }

Maximum (Row Minimum)= 1

Maximini Value = 1

and Column Maximum = { 5, 3, 1, 5, 6 }

Minimum (Column Maximum)= 1

Minimax Value= 1

(B) For Mixed strategy:

(i) 2×2 Games without saddle point:

Consider 2×2 two person zero sum game without any saddle point having the payoff matrix for player A.

	B_1	B_2
A_1	a_{11}	a_{12}
A_2	a_{21}	a_{22}

The optimum mixed strategies

$$S_A = \begin{vmatrix} A_1 & A_2 \\ p_1 & p_2 \end{vmatrix}$$

$$S_B = \begin{vmatrix} B_1 & B_2 \\ q_1 & q_2 \end{vmatrix}$$

where

$$p_1 = \frac{(a_{22} - a_{21})}{(a_{11} + a_{22}) - (a_{12} + a_{21})} \qquad p_1 + p_2 = 1 \;\Rightarrow\; p_2 = 1 - p_1$$

$$q_1 = \frac{(a_{22} - a_{12})}{(a_{11} + a_{22}) - (a_{12} + a_{21})} \qquad q_1 + q_2 = 1 \;\Rightarrow\; q_2 = 1 - q_1$$

The value of game $(\upsilon) = \dfrac{a_{11}a_{22} - a_{12}a_{21}}{(a_{11} + a_{22}) - (a_{12} + a_{21})}$

Example: Solve the following game and determine the value of the game

$$A \overset{B}{\begin{vmatrix} 5 & 1 \\ 3 & 4 \end{vmatrix}}$$

Solution:

$$A \overset{B}{\begin{vmatrix} 5 & 1 \\ 3 & 4 \end{vmatrix}}$$ after the comparison from the general format of the matrix.

$$A \overset{B}{\begin{vmatrix} 5 & 1 \\ 3 & 4 \end{vmatrix}} \approx \begin{matrix} & B_1 & B_2 \\ A_1 & a_{11} & a_{12} \\ A_2 & a_{21} & a_{22} \end{matrix}$$

$a_{11} = 5$ $\quad a_{12} = 1$ $\quad a_{21} = 3$ $\quad a_{22} = 4$

The optimum mixed strategies are

where

$$S_A \begin{vmatrix} A_1 & A_2 \\ p_1 & p_2 \end{vmatrix} \text{ and } S_a \begin{vmatrix} B_1 & B_2 \\ q_1 & q_2 \end{vmatrix}$$

$$p_1 = \frac{a_{22} - a_{21}}{(a_{11} + a_{22}) - (a_{12} + a_{21})} = \frac{4-3}{(5+4)-(1+3)} = \frac{1}{5}$$

$p_2 = 1 - p_1 = 1 - 1/5 = 4/5$

$$q_1 = \frac{a_{22} - a_{12}}{(a_{11} + a_{22}) - (a_{12} + a_{21})} = \frac{4-1}{(5+4)-(1+3)} = \frac{3}{5}$$

$q_2 = 1 - q_1 = 1 - 3/5 = 2/5$

$$\text{Value of Game}(v) = \frac{(5\times4)-(1\times3)}{(5+4)-(1+3)} = \frac{17}{5}$$

$S_A = (1/5, 4/5)$ $\qquad$ $S_B = (3/5, 2/5)$

Dominance Rule: The size of the pay-off matrix can be reduced by applying dominance rule. It is helpful for converting any size of matrix into the size 2×2, m×2 or 2×n.

Principle of Dominance Rule: If one pure strategy of a player is better or superior than another one, then the inferior strategy may be simply ignored by assigning a zero probability by searching for optimal strategies.

Procedure of Dominance Rule:

Rule 1: If each element in one row say r^{th} of the pay-off matrix $[V_{ij}]$, is less than or equal to corresponding element in the other row, say s^{th} , then the player A never choosing r^{th} strategy. Such r^{th} row is said to be dominated by the sth row.

OR

If for all j=1, 2,........n and $V_{rj} \leq V_{sj}$, then the probability x_r of choosing r^{th} strategy will be zero.

Rule 2: Similarly, if each element in one column, say p^{th} column is greater than or equal to the corresponding element in the other column q^{th}, then the player B will never choosing p^{th} strategy. Such p^{th} column is said to be dominated by q^{th} column.

OR

If for all i=1, 2,........n and $V_{ip} >= V_{iq}$, then the probability x_p of choosing p^{th} strategy will be zero.

Rule 3: Dominated rows and column may be deleted to reduce the size of pay-off matrix as the optimal strategies will remain unaffected.

Rule 4: Dominance need not be based on the superiority of pure strategies only. A given strategy can be dominated if it is inferior to an average of two or more other pure strategies. In general, if some convex linear combination of some rows dominates the ith row, then the ith row will be deleted. If the ith row dominates the convex linear combination of some other rows, then one of the rows involving in the combination may be deleted. Similar arguments for columns also.

Example: Solve the following game with the help of dominance rule.

		B		
		I	II	III
	I	-4	6	3
A	II	-3	-3	4
	III	2	-3	4

Solution:

Step 1 : It is clear that from the matrix this game has no saddle point.

Step2: In the above matrix, it is clear that all the element of the III column is greater than the I column elements of the matrix from player's B point of view. Thus III column is dominated by I column, then the reduced matrix is given below:

		B	
		I	II
	I	-4	6
A	II	-3	-3
	III	2	-3

Step 3. Again if the reduce matrix is looked from A's point of view, it is clear that II row is dominated by III row.

		B	
		I	II
A	I	-4	6
	II	2	-3

		B	
		B_1	B_2
A	A_1	a_{11}	a_{12}
	A_2	a_{21}	a_{22}

$a_{11}=-4$ $\quad a_{12}=6$ $\quad a_{21}=2$ $\quad a_{22}=-3$

$$p_1=\frac{(a_{22}-a_{21})}{(a_{11}+a_{22})-(a_{12}+a_{21})}=\frac{(-3-2)}{(-4-3)-(6+2)}=\frac{1}{3}$$

$p_2= 1\text{-}1/3= 2/3$

$$q_1=\frac{(a_{22}-a_{12})}{(a_{11}+a_{22})-(a_{12}+a_{21})}=\frac{(-3-6)}{(-4-3)-(6+2)}=\frac{3}{5}$$

$q_2= 1\text{-}q_1= 1\text{-}3/5 = 2/5$

$$v=\frac{(a_{11}a_{22})-(a_{21}a_{12})}{(a_{11}+a_{22})-(a_{12}+a_{21})}=\frac{(-4)(-3)-(2)(6)}{(-4-3)-(6+2)}=0$$

Thus, the outcome is following:

1) The player A chooses mixed strategy $(X_1, X_2, X_3) = (1/3, 0, 2/3)$.
2) The player B chooses mixed strategy $(Y_1, Y_2, Y_3) = (3/5, 2/5, 0)$.
3) The value of the game is zero i.e. the game is fair.

2 x n or m x 2 games (Graphical Method)

Let us consider that 2 x n games

$$A \begin{array}{c|ccc|} & B_1 & B_2 \ldots & B_n \\ A_1 & a_{11} & a_{12} & a_{1n} \\ A_2 & a_{21} & a_{22} & a_{2n} \end{array}$$

Suppose that the mixed strategy for player A be given by

$$SA = \begin{pmatrix} A_1 & A_2 \\ p_1 & p_2 \end{pmatrix} \text{ such that } p_1 + p_2 = 1, p_1, p_2 \geq 0$$

Now for each of the pure strategies available to B, expected pay off for player A would be as follows:

The player B would like to choose that pure move B_j against S_A for which $E_j(p)$ is a minimum for j = 1,2 ...n. Let us denote this

B_1	$E_1(p) = a_{11} p_1 + a_{21} p_2$
B_2	$E_2(p) = a_{12} p_1 + a_{22} p_2$
B_3	$E_3(p) = a_{13} p_1 + a_{23} p_2$
:	:
:	:
B_n	$E_n(p) = a_{1n} p_1 + a_{2n} p_2$

minimum expected pay off for A by

$v = \text{Min}(E_j(p)), j = 1, 2.....n$

The objective of player A is to selecte p_1 and p_2 in such a way that v is as large as possible. This may be done by plotting the straight lines.

$E_j(p) = a_{1j}p_1 - a_{2j}p_2$

$= (a_{1j} - a_{2j})\, p_1 + a_{2j}$

$j = 1,2........n$

as linear functions of p_1.

The highest point of the lower boundary of these lines will give maximum value among the minimum expected payoff's on the lower boundary (lower envelop) and the optimum value of probability P_1 and P_2. Now the two strategies of player B corresponding to those lines which pass through the maximum point can be determined. It helps in reducing the size of the game to (2 x 2).

Similarly, we can determine the m x 2 game in the same way and get minimax point which will be the lowest point on the upper boundary (upper envelops).

Graphical Method .

Example 1. Solve the following 2 x 3 game graphically.

Solution : Let the mixed strategy for player A be given by

		Player B	
	1	3	11
Player A	8	5	2

$$S_A = \begin{pmatrix} A_1 & A_2 \\ p_1 & p_2 \end{pmatrix} \text{ with } p_2 = 1 - p_1 \text{ against player B.}$$

The A's expected pay off against B's pure move is given by

These expected payoff equations are then plotted as functions

Bs pure move	As expected payoff $E(p_1)$
B1	$E(p_1) = p_1 + 8\,(1-p_1) = -7p_1 + 8$
B2	$E(p_2) = 3p_1 + 5\,(1-p_1) = -7p_1 + 8$
B2	$E(p_3) = 11p_1 + 2\,(1-p_1) = 9p_1 + 2$

of P1, which shows the payoffs of each column represented as points on two vertical axes 1 and 2.

Unit of distance apart.

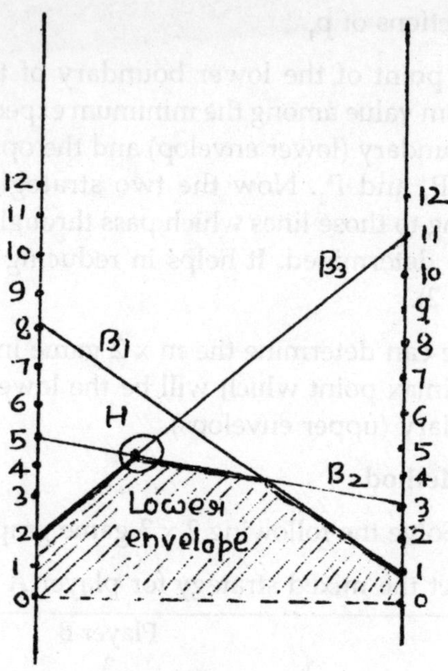

Now since the player A wishes to maximize his minimum expected payoff, we consider the highest point of intersection H on the lower envelope of A's expected payoff equation. The lines B2 and B3 passing through H define the relevant moves B2 and B3 that alone need to play.

The solution to the origin 2 x 3 games reduced to

$$\begin{array}{c} \\ A_1 \\ A_2 \end{array}\begin{array}{c} \begin{array}{cc} B_2 & B_3 \end{array} \\ \left[\begin{array}{cc} 3 & 11 \\ 5 & 2 \end{array}\right] \end{array}$$

The optimum strategy for A and B is given by

$$S_A = \begin{pmatrix} A_1 & A_2 \\ p_1 & p_2 \end{pmatrix} \; p_1 + p_2 = 1$$

$$S_B = \begin{pmatrix} B_1 & B_2 & B_3 \\ o & q_1 & q_2 \end{pmatrix} \; q_1 + q_2 = 1$$

$$p_1 = \frac{2-5}{3+2-(11+5)} = \frac{-3}{-11} = \frac{3}{11}$$

$$p_2 = 1 - p1 = 1 - = \left(\frac{3}{11}\right) = \frac{8}{11}$$

$$q_1 = \frac{2-11}{-11} = \frac{-9}{-11} = \frac{9}{11}$$

$$q_2 = 1 - \frac{9}{11} = \frac{2}{11}$$

$$S_A = \left(\frac{3}{11}, \frac{8}{11}\right), S_B = \left(0, \frac{9}{11}, \frac{2}{11}\right)$$

$$\text{Value of game}(\gamma) = \frac{6-55}{-11} = \frac{49}{11}$$

8.8 Practice Problems:

1. What do you mean by Game theory?
2. Describe the types of Game?
3. Explain the basic term used in game theory?
4. Explain the Game model?
5. Describe the characteristics of competitive game?
6. Explain the dominance rule for Game theory?
7. How dominance rule is useful for solving the problem?
8. Write the short notes on following.
   (i) Strategy

(ii) Payoff matrix
(iii) The Minimax-Maximin principles
(iv) Saddle point
(v) Principles of Dominance

9. Solve the following game.

(a)

		B		
		B_1	B_2	B_3
	A_1	1	3	1
A	A_2	0	- 4	-3
	A_3	1	5	-1

(b)

		B	
		B_1	B_2
A	A1	-5	2
	A2	-7	-4

(c)

		B				
		I	II	III	IV	V
	I	-2	0	0	5	3
A	II	3	2	1	2	2
	III	-4	-3	0	-2	6
	IV	5	3	-4	2	-6

(d)

		B	
		b_1	b_2
A	a1	1	1
	a2	4	-3

(e)

		B			
		b_1	b_2	b_3	b_4
	a_1	- 5	2	0	7
a	a_2	5	6	4	8
	a_3	4	0	2	-3

(f)

		B		
		1	2	3
A	a1	-1	2	-2
	a2	6	4	-6

10. Solve the game whose payoff matrix is given below.

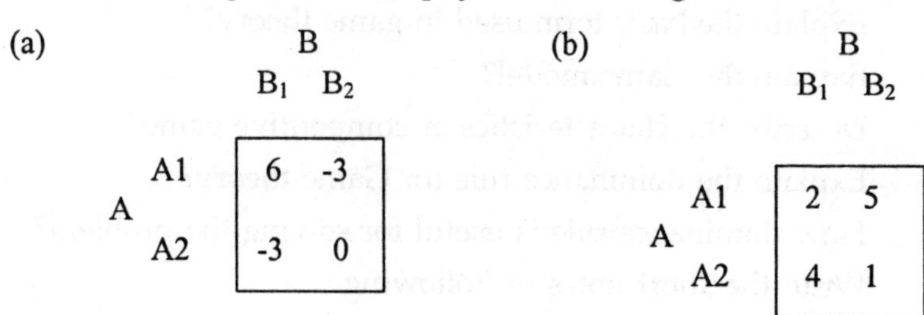

(a)

		B	
		B_1	B_2
A	A1	6	-3
	A2	-3	0

(b)

		B	
		B_1	B_2
A	A1	2	5
	A2	4	1

(c)

		B	
		B_1	B_2
A	A1	4	-4
	A2	-4	4

(d)

		B	
		B_1	B_2
A	A1	5	1
	A2	3	4

11. Solve the following 2 × 3 game graphically.

(c)

1	1	-3
2	3	5
3	-1	6
4	4	1
5	2	2
6	-5	0

[Ans. V= 17/5 , S_A=(0,3/5,0,2/5,0,0) S_B=(4/5,1/5)]

(d)

		B		
		1	2	3
A	a1	1	3	1
	a2	8	5	2

[Ans. V= 49/11 , S_A= (3/11 ,8/11) S_B = (0,9/11,2/11)]

(c)

		B	
		I	II
A	(i)	1	2
	(ii)	5	7
	(iii)	-7	9
	(iv)	-4	-3
	(v)	2	1

(d)

	PlayerB		
Player A	-4	-3	3
	-3	1	1

12. Solve the following game by using dominance rule.

(a)

		B		
		b_1	b_2	b_3
a	a_1	3	-2	4
	a_2	-1	4	2
	a_3	2	2	6

(b)

		B		
		1	2	3
A	a1	1	7	2
	a2	6	2	7
	a3	5	1	6

(c)

	B			
I	-5	-10	9	0
II	6	7	8	1
III	8	7	15	1
IV	3	4	-1	4

(d)

	B			
	1	7	3	4
A	5	6	4	5
	7	2	0	3

Objective Question

1. Assignment problem is basically a
   (a) Maximization Problem
   (b) Minimization Problem
   (c) Transportation Problem
   (d) Primal Problem

2. The assignment Problem is Solved by
   (a) Simplex Method
   (b) Graphical method
   (c) Vector Method
   (d) Hungarian Method

3. In Hungarian method of solving assignment problem, the row opportunity cost matrix is obtained by:
   (a) Dividing each row by the elements of the row above.
   (b) Subtracting the element of the row from the elements of the row above it.
   (c) Subtracting the smallest element from all other elements of the row.
   (d) Subtracting all the elements of the row from the highest element in the matrix.

4. The horizontal and vertical lines drawn to cover all zeros of the matrix must be:
   (a) equal to each other
   (b) Equal to m × n
   (c) Equal to m+n
   (d) Number of rows or column.

5. The assignment matrix is always
   (a) Rectangular Matrix
   (b) Square Matrix
   (c) Identity Matrix
   (d) None of the above

6. To balance an assignment matrix we have to
   (a) Open a dummy row
   (b) Open a dummy column
   (c) Open either a dummy row or column depending upon the situation.
   (d) We can not balance the assignment problem.

Chapter **9**

Replacement Problem

Course outline

9.1 Introduction

9.2 The Replacement Situations

9.3 Cost associated with Maintenance

9.4 Replacement Policy

9.5 Replacement of items that deteriorates with time.

Case. 1. Replacement of items whose maintenance cost increases with time and the value of money remains same dunning the period.

Case.2. Replacement of items whose maintenance cost increases with time and the value of money also changes with time

9.6 Replacement of items that fails suddenly and completely.

9.7 Practice problems

9.1 Introduction

Replacement problem arise when equipment need replacement due to their decreased efficiency, failure or breakdown.

There are the following reasons which demand the replacement of certain items.

1. The old item has become inefficient or requires expensive maintenance cost.
2. The odd item has failed due to any defect.
3. A new item has been introduced due to improve technology.

The main objective of replacement is to direct the organization for maximizing its project (or minimizing the cost).

9.2 The Replacement situations

The replacement situations may be divided into four categories:-

1. Replacement of capital item that deteriorates with time e.g. machine, buses, tracks etc.
2. Replacement of item is anticipation of complete failure, the probability of which increases with time.
3. Problems in mortality and staffing.
4. Replacement of an equipment (or item) may be necessary due to new researches otherwise the system may become out of data.

9.3 Cost associated with maintenance

There are various cost associated with maintenance. The objective is to minimize the maintenance cost.

a. Purchase cost or capital cost (C):-

The cost is incurred at the beginning of the life of the machine i.e at the time of purchasing the machine or equipment.

b. Salvage value/scrap value/ Resale valve/Depreciation (S):-

As the age of machine increases, the resale value decrease as its operating efficiency decreases and the maintenance costs increase. It depends upon the operating conditions of the machine and life of the machine

c. Running cost including maintenance, Repair and operating costs

There costs are the functions of age of the machine and usage of the machine. As the usage increases or the age increases, due to were and tear, many components fail to work and they are to be replaced. The different cost curve is given below:

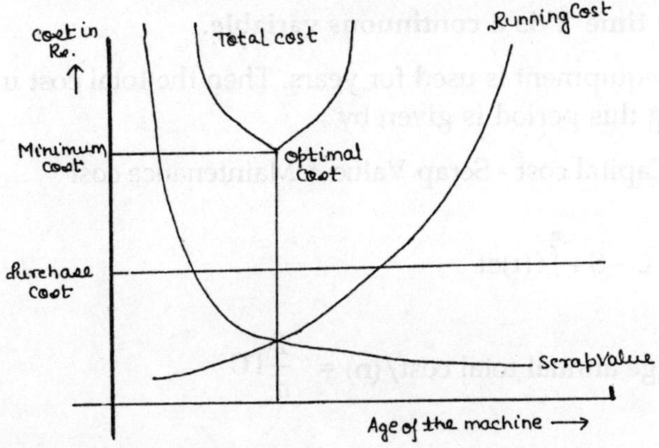

9.4 Replacement policy

Future is not certain, therefore we can't predict the time of failure of an item exactly. During the maintenance period, there may be the requirement of only minor repairs or maintenance but there could also be the requirement or replacement of parts (Components). Thus we have to formulate the replacement policy for the replacement of any equipment, machine or persons etc.

1. Replacement of item whose efficiency deteriorates with time.
2. Replacement of item that fail suddenly and completely.
3. Replacement due to change in technology or the process.

9.5 Replacement of items that deteriorate with time

In general, the cost of maintenance of certain items increases with time and at one stage these costs become so high that it is more economical to replace the item by a new one.

Case (1) Replacement of items whose maintenance cost increases with time and the value of money remain same during the period.

Let us consider that

C is the capital cost of equipment.

S is the scrap value of an equipment.

N is the number of years the equipment would be in use.

F (t): maintenance cost function w.r.t. time.

A (n): Average total annual cost.

When time 't' is a continuous variable.

It the equipment is used for years. Then the total cost incurred during this period is given by

TC= Capital cost - Scrap Value + Maintenance cost

$$= C - S + \int^{n} f(t)dt$$

$$\text{Average annual total cost}/(n) = \frac{1}{n}TC$$

$$= \frac{C-S}{n} + \frac{1}{n}\int_{o}^{n} f(t)dt$$

For minimum Cost,

$$\text{We have } \frac{d}{dn}(A(n)) = 0$$

$$\frac{-(c-s)}{n^2} - \frac{1}{n^2}\int_{o}^{n} f(t)dt + \frac{1}{n}f(n) = o$$

$$f(n) = \frac{c-s}{n} + \frac{1}{n}\int_{o}^{n} f(t).dt$$

= A (n)

clearly

$$\frac{d^2}{dn^2}A(n) =\geq o$$

at $f(n) = A(n)$

This suggests that the equipment should be replaced when the maintenance cost equals the average annual total cost. Case (II) when time 't' is a discrete variable:

For discrete value of 't', n is optimal at the average annual cost. This suggests the optimal replacement policy. According be which:

$$F(n) = \frac{1}{n}[c - s(t) + \sum_{0}^{n} f(t)]$$

1. **Replace the equipment at the end of n years, if the maintenance cost in the (n+1)th, year. is more than the average total cost in the nth year.**
2. **Do not replace the equipment if the current year's maintenance cost is less than the pervious year's total cost.**

Example 1: The cost of a truck is Rs 3000. The salvage value (resale Value) and the running cost are even as under. Find the most economical replacement age of the buck.

Year	1	2	3	4	5	6	7
Running cost	600	700	800	900	1000	1200	1500
Resale Value	2000	1333	1000	750	500	300	300

Solution. To find the average cost per year of the machine, we prepare the following table:

Age of Replacement in year's	Table Running cost (Rs)	Depreciation = Cost of Truck – Resale price Rs	Total cost Rs	Average cost per year
1	600	1000	1600	1600
2	1300	1667	2967	1483.5
3	2100	2000	4100	1366.67
4	3000	2250	5250	1312.50
5	4000	2500	6500	(1300.00)*
6	5200	2700	7900	1316.67
7	6700	2700	9400	1342.86

It is clear from the table, that the average cost per year decrease up to the end of 5th year and then this cost begin to increase. Hence the lowest average cost per year is achieved by replacing the truck at the end of every 5 year.

Example. 2 The cost of machine is Rs 6100 and its scrap value (resale Value) is only Rs 100 experience to be under.

Years	1	2	3	4	5	6	7	8
Maintenance cost in Rs	100	250	400	600	900	1250	1600	2000

When should the machine be replaced?

Solution. We have given the running cost f (n), the scrap value S= Rs 100 and the cost of the machine C = Rs 6100. In order to determine the optimal time n when the machine should be replaced, we calculate an average.

Year (1)	Running cost (2)	Cumulative Running cost ? f(n) (3)	Depreciation cost (C-S) (4)	Total cost (5)=3+4	Average cost Per year (Rs)
1	100	100	6000	6100	6100
2	250	350	6000	6350	3175
3	400	750	6000	6750	2250
4	600	1350	6000	7350	1837.5
5	900	2250	6000	8250	1650
6	1250	3500	6000	9500	(1583.33)*
7	1600	5100	6000	11100	1585.71
8	2000	7100	6000	13100	1637.50

It is clear from the table, that lowest average cost per year is achieved by replacing the machine at the end of 6th year.

Example.3 A machine costs Rs. 10,000. Its operating cost and resale values are given below:

Year	1	2	3	4	5	6	7	8
Operating cost	1000	1200	1400	1700	2000	2500	9000	3500
Resale Value	6000	4000	3200	2600	2500	2400	2000	1600

Determine at what time it could be replaced?

Solution:- Given the cost of equipment (c) = 10000. To determine the optimal time n, when the equipment should be replaced, we calculate an average total cost per year as shown in the following table:

1 Year	2 f (n)	3 Σf (n)	4 S	5 c - s	6=3+5 TC=(C-S+ Σf (n))	7=6/1 A(n)=Tc/n
1	1000	1000	6000	4000	5000	500
2	1200	2200	4000	6000	8200	4100
3	1400	3600	3200	6800	10400	3466.7
4	1700	5300	2600	7400	12700	3175
5	2000	7300	2500	7500	14700	2940
6	2500	9800	2400	7600	17400	(2900)*
7	3000	12800	2000	8000	20800	2971.4
8	3500	16300	1600	8400	24700	3089.7

From the table, it is clear that the average annual x cost is minimum at the end of the 6th year (Rs. 2900), we conclude that the equipment should be replaced at the end of 6th year.

Example:-

a. Machine A costs Rs. 9000. Annual operating costs are Rs. 200 for the first year, and then increased by Rs. 2000 every year. Determine the best age to replace the machine. If the optimum replacement policy is fallowed, what will be the average yearly cost of the owning and operating the machine?

b. Machine B costs Rs.10000. Annual operating costs are Rs. 400 for the first year and then increased by Rs. 800 every year. You now have a machine of type A which is one year old. Should you replace it with B, if so when?

Solution:- We prepare a table to find the average cost per year for machine A.

Year	Running cost	Total running cost	Depreciation value (c-s)	TC=C-S+? f(n)	A(n)
1	2	3	4	5=3+4	6=5/1
1	200	200	9000	9200	9200
2	2200	2400	9000	11400	5700
3	4200	6600	9000	15600	(5200)*
4	6200	12800	9000	21800	5450

Since the average annual cost is minimum at the end of 3rd year, the optimum time of replacement is 3 years. The average yearly cost of owning and operating machine is Rs. 5200.

Now we find the average yearly cost for the machine B in the following table:

Year	Running cost	Total running cost	Depreciation value (c-s)	TC= $C-S+\Sigma f(n)$	A(n)
1	2	3	4	5=3+4	6=5/1
1	400	400	10000	10400	10400
2	1200	1600	10000	11600	5800
3	2000	3600	10000	13600	4533.33
4	2800	6400	10000	16400	4100
5	3600	10000	10000	20000	(4000)*
6	4400	14400	10000	24400	4066.66

Since the minimum average cost is Rs. 4000 for machine B and less than the average cost of Rs. 5200 for machine A, so A can be replaced by machine B.

Machine B can be purchased when the cost for next year of running the machine A exceeds the average yearly cost for machine B.

The total yearly cost for machine A is as follows:

For 1st year = 11400-9200 = 2200 < 4000

2nd year = 15600-11400 = 4200 > 4000

3rd year = 21800-9200 = 6200 < 4000

Hence, we observe that the cost Rs 2200 for one year old machine A will not exceed the lowest average cost Rs 4000 for B until the second year.

Therefore, machine A should be replaced with machine B after one year from now, before it reaches the normal replacement age of three years.

Case 2. Replacement of items whose maintenance costs increases with time and value of money also changes with time.

A. Money Value:-

The value of money changes with time, Suppose a person borrows Rs 100 at the interest of 10% per year then after one year we have to return rupees 110. Thus Rs 110 after one year from now are equivalent to Rs 100 today. Thus, we can say that the value of money changes with time.

B. Present Value or Present worth:

If are is the rate of interest then $(1+r)^{-n}$ is called the present worth factor or present value of one rupee spent in n years a time from now. The expression $(1+r)^{-n}$ is known as the payment compound amount factor of one rupee spent is n years duration.

C. Discount rate (or Depreciation ratio):-

The value money decreases with a constant ratio which is known as its discount rate or depreciation ratio. If r is the rate of interest per year on Rs 1.00. Then the present value of Rs 1.00 to be spent after one year from now is Rs $\frac{1}{1+r}$ this ratio $v = \frac{1}{1+r}$ is the discount rate.

Theorem:- If the maintenance cost increases with time and the value of money decreases with constant rate i.e depreciation value is given. The replacement policy will be:

A. Replace if the running cost of next period is greater than the weighted average of previous cost.

B. Do not replace if the running cost of next period is less than the weighted average of previous costs.

Proof:- For proof of the above statement students are advised to refer to operations research books with mathematical approach.

Note:- The reweighted average expenditure is given by:

$$\omega(n) = \frac{\left\{C + \sum_{i=1}^{n} R_i d^{i-1}\right\}}{\sum_{i=1}^{n} d^{i-1}}$$

Where, n is the period, i = year d = discount factor C= capital expenditure

$$Rn < \omega(n) < R_{n+1}$$

The optimum replacement age must satisfy the above conditions.

Example 1: The yearly cost of two machines A and B, when money value is neglected is shown is the table given below. Find their cost pattern if money value is 10% per year and hence find which machine is more economical.

Year	1	2	3
Machine A (Rs).	1800	1200	1400
Machine B (Rs)	2800	200	1400

Solution:- When the value of money is 10% per year, the discount rate i.e :

$$d = (1/1+i) + (1/1+0.1) = 0.9091$$

The discounting table for machine A and B are as fallows:

Year	1	2	3	Total cost (Rs)
Machine (A) Discounted	1800	1200x0.9091 =1090.9	$1400x(0.9091)^2$ =1157.04	4047.94
Machine (B) Discounted	2800	200x0.9091 =181.82	$1400x(0.9091)^2$ =1157.04	4138.86

The table shows that the total cost of machine A is less than that of machine B. Hence, Machine A is more economical when money value is changing.

Example 2: A machine costs Rs 500/ - operation and maintenance costs are zero for the first year and increase by Rs 100-every year. If money worth 5% every day, determine the best age at which the machine should be replaced. The resale value of the machine is negligibly small. What is the weighted average cast of owing and operating the machine?

Solution.

$$\text{Discount Rate (a)} = (d) = \frac{1}{1+i}$$

$$= \frac{1}{1+0.05} = 0.9524$$

Weighted average cost:-

Year of Service (n)	Mainte-nance cost R_i (Rs)	Discount factor (d^{i-1})	Discounted Mainte-nance cost $R_i x d^{i-1}$ (Rs)	Total cost $\left(C+\sum_{i=1}^{n} R_i d^{i-1}\right)$	Cumulative discount factor $\left(\sum_{i=1}^{n} d^{i-1}\right)$	weighted average annual cost w(n) = $\left(\frac{\left\{C+\sum_{i=1}^{n} R_i d^{i-1}\right\}}{\sum_{i=1}^{n} d^{i-1}}\right)$
1	0	1.000	0	0	1	500.00
2	100	0.9524	95:24	595:24	1.9524	304.88
3	200	0.9010	181.4	776.64	2.8594	217.61
4.	300	0.8678	259.14	1035.78	3.7232	278.20
5	400	0.8277	320.08	136486	4.5459	300.25

Since 200 < 217.61 < 300 i.e W (3) = Rs 2'17.61 > R_3= Rs200 and W(3) = Rs '217.61 < R_4 = Rs 300.

Hence, the machine is to be replaced at the end of 3rd year. The weighted Average cost of running the machine is Rs 217.61.

9.6 Replacement of items that fails suddenly and completely

It is very difficult to predict that a particular equipment will fail at a particular time uncertainty can be avoided by deriving the probability distribution of failures. Here it is assumed that the failure occurs only at the end of the period, say t.

Thus the objective becomes to find the value of t which minimize the total cost involved for the replacement.

Mortality Tables.

These tables are used to drive the probability distribution of life span of equipment in question.

Let M(t) = number of survivors at any time t.

M (t-1) = number of survivors at any time (t-1).

N = initial number of equipments.

Then the probability of failure during time period t is given by

$$P(t) = \frac{M(t-1) - M(t)}{N}$$

The probability that an equipment has survived to an age (t-1) and will fail during the interval (t-1) to t can be defined as the conditional probability of failure. It is given by

$$P(t) = \frac{M(t-1) - M(t)}{M(t-1)}$$

The probability of survival to an age t is given by

$$Ps(t) = \frac{M(t)}{N}$$

We shall consider the following two types of replacement policy-

1. **Individual Replacement Policy**

Under this policy an item is replaced immediately after it fails.

2. **Group replacement policy.**

Let all the items in a system be replaced after a time interval with provisions that individuate replacement can be made if any item fails during this time period.

Group replacement must be made at the end of tth period if the cost of individual replacements for the tth period is greater than the average cost per period through the end of t periods. Group replacement is not possible at the end of period t if the cost of individual replacement at the (t-1) end period is less than the average cost per period through the end of t period.

Example:- Calculate the probability of failure of an item in good condition in each month from the fallowing survival table:

Months Number (t)	0	0	1	2	3	4	6	7	8	9	10
original number of items working at the end of each year	1000	940	820	580	400	280	190	130	70	30	0

Solution:- Here 't' is the number of Months M (t) is the number of items i.e items in good condition at the end of tth month. The probability of failure in each month is calculated as under.

Year (t)	Item in good condition M (t)	Probability of items that fail in t^{th} year = { M(t^{-1})- M(t)}/N
0	1000	—
1	940	(1000-940)/1000=0.06
2	820	(940-820)/1000=0.12
3	580	(820-580)/1000=0.24
4	400	(580-400)/1000=0.18
5	280	(400-280)/1000=0.12
6	190	(280-190)/1000=0.09
7	130	(190-130)/1000=0.06
8	70	(130-70)/1000=0.06
9	30	(70-30)/1000=0.04
10	0	(30-0)/1000=0.03

Example 2: A system consists of 1000 electric bulbs when any bulb fails, it is replaced immediately and the cost of replacing a bulb individuality is Rs 2 only. of all the bulbs are replaced at the same time, the cost per bulb will be Rs 50 paisa per bulb.

Week	1	2	3	4	5
% failing by the end of week	10	25	50	80	100

Step 1. P_1 be the probability that a bulb which was new when placed in position per use, pails during the i [th] week of its life.

$P_1 = 0.15$

$P_2 = 0.25 - 0.1 = 0.15$

$P_3 = 0.5 - 0.25 = 0.25$

$P_4 = 0.8 - 0.5 = 0.3$

$P_5 = 1 - 0.8 = 0.2$

$\Sigma P_1 = 0.1 + 0.15 + 0.25 + 0.3 + 0.2 = 1$

Step 2. Let N_i be the number of replacement at the end of the tth week.

No = Number of items in the beginning.

= 1000

N_1 = N0P1 = 1000 x 0.1 = 100

N_2 = N0P2 + N1 P1 = 15.0 + 10 = 160

N_3 = No P3 + N1 P2 + N2 P1

= 11000x(0.25) + 100x (0.15) + 160x0.1 = 276

N_4 = No P4 + N1 P3 + N2 P2 +N3 P1

=1000 x (0.3) + 100 x (0.25) + 160 (0.15) + 276 (0.1)

= 376.6

N_5 = No P5 + N1 P4 + N2 P3 + N3 P2 + N4 P1

= 1000 (0.2) = 100 (0.3) + 160 (0.25) + 276 (0.15) + 376.6 (0.1) = 349.06

Step 3. We calculate the expected life of each

$$\text{bulb} = \sum_{1-1}^{5} iPi$$

$= 1 \times 0.1 + 2 \times 0.15 + 3 \times 0.25 + 4 \times 0.3 + 5 \times 0.2$

$= 3.35$

Average number of failure per week.

$= \frac{1000}{3.35} = 298.5 = 299$ (approximately)

Step 4. The cost of individual replacement

= 299 x 2 = Rs 598

End of week	Individual replacement	Total cost Rs (Individual + group)	Average Cost
1.	100	100 x 2 + 1000 x 0.5 = 700	700
2.	100 + 160 = 260	260 x 2 + 1000 x 0.5 = 1020	(510)*
3.	260 + 281 = 541	541 x 2 + 1000 x 0.5 = 1582	527.33
4.	541 + 379 =920	920 x 2 +1000 x 0.5 = 2340	585
5.	920 + 350 = 1270	1270 x 2 + 1000 x 0.5 = 3040	608

The average cost is minimum in the 2nd week; the optimal replacement period to have a group replacement is after every 2nd week. Since the average cost is less than Rs 598 for individual replacement, the group replacement policy is preferable.

Example.3 The probability P_n of failure just before age is shown below. If individual replacement costs Rs. 12.5 and group replacement costs Rs 3 per item. Find the optimal replacement policy.

N	1	2	3	4	5
P_n	0.1	0.2	0.25	0.3	0.15

Solution. Step 1. Set Pi be the probability of failure during the ith period.

$P_1 = 0.1\ P_2 = 0.2\ P_3 = 0.25\ P_A = 0.3\ P_5 = 0.15$

Sit total number of items = 1000

No = 1000

$N_1 = N_oP_1 = 1000 \times 0.1 = 100$

$N_2 = N_oP_2 + N_1P_1 = 1000 \times 0.2 + 100 \times 0.1 = 210$

$N_3 = NoP_3 + N_1P_2 + N_2P_1 = 1000 \times 0.25 + 100 \times 0.2 + 210 \times 0.1 = 291$

$N_4 = NoP_4 + N_1P_3 + N_2P_2 + N_3P_1 = 1000 \times 0.3\ 100 \times 0.25 + 210 \times 0.2 + 291 \times 0.1 = 396.1$

$N_5 = N_oP_5 + N_1P_4 + N_2P_3 + N_3P_2 + N_4P_1 = 1000 \times 0.15\ 100 \times 0.3 + 210 \times 0.25 + 291 \times 0.2 + 396 \times 0.1 = 330$

Step 2. Expected life of each item = $\sum_{1-1}^{5} iPi$

$= 1\times 0.1 + 2 \times 0.2 + 3 \times 0.25$

$+ 4 \times 0.3 + 5\ 0.15$

$= 1\times0.1 + 2\times0.2 + 3\times0.25 + 4\times0.3 + 5\times0.15$

$= 3912.50$

End of period	Individual replacement	Total Cost (Individual + group	Average Cost
1	100	100 x 12.5 + 1000 x 3 = 4250	4250
2	100+210=310	310x12.5+1000x3=6875	(3437.05)*
3	310+291=601	601X12.5+1000X3=10512.5	3504.166

Since the average cost is minimum at the end of 2nd period, we replace all the items simultaneously after every 2nd period. Also the average cost of group replacement policy is less than that of individual replacement Rs 3912.5. Hence prefer group replacement policy.

9.7 Practice Problems

1. What is replacement? Describe some important replacement situations.

2. Discuss the problem on replacement of items that fail completely.
3. Write short notes on replacement models.
4. What type of cost associated with maintenance of machines?
5. Explain the replacement policies.
6. The cost of a machine is Rs. 5000. The running cost and the salvage value of the machine are given as under. Find the optimal replacement policy.

Year	1	2	3	4	5	6	7	8
Running Cost in Rs.	1500	1600	1800	2100	2500	2900	3400	4000
Salvage Value in Rs.	3500	2500	1700	1200	800	500	500	500

Salvage value means the cost at which the machine could be sold at the end of the year.

7. A firm considering when to replace its machine whose price is 12200. The scrap value of the machine is Rs. 200 only. From past experience the maintenance costs of the machine are as under:

Year	1	2	3	4	5	6	7	8
Maintenance Cost in Rs.	200	500	800	1200	1800	2500	3200	4000

Find when the new machine should be purchased.

8. The cost per year of running a truck whose purchase price is Rs. 30000 are as follows. Determine when is the replacement due.

Year	1	2	3	4	5	6	7
Running Cost (Rs.)	5000	6000	7000	9000	11500	14000	17000
Resale Value (Rs)	15000	7500	3750	1875	1000	1000	1000

9. The cost of a truck is Rs 3500. The salvage value and the running costs are given below. Find the most economical age for replacement.

Year	1	2	3	4	5	6	7
Running Cost (Rs.)	600	700	800	900	1000	1200	1500
Resale Value (Rs)	2500	1833	1500	1250	1000	800	800

10. A truck is priced at Rs. 60000 and running costs are estimated at Rs. 6000 for each of the first four years, increasing by Rs. 2000 per year in the fifty and subsequent years. If money it worth 10% per year, when should the truck will be replaced? Assume that the truck will eventually be sold for scrap at a negligible price.
11. A machine cost Rs. 10000 operating costs Rs 500 per year for the first five years. In the sixth and succeeding years operating costs increases by Rs 100 per year. Assuming a 10% discount rate of money per year, find the optimal length of time to hold the machine before we replace it.
12. A computer contains 10000 resistors. When any one of the resistors fails. It is replaced. The cost of replacing a single resistor is Rs. 1 only. If all resistors are replaced at the same time, the cost per resistor would be reduced to 35 paise. The per cent surviving by the end of month 't' is as

Month	0	1	2	3	4	5	6
% surving by the end of month	100	97	90	70	30	15	0

follows:

What is the optimum plan?

13. There are 1000 bulbs in the system, survival rate is given

Week	0	1	2	3	4
Bulbs in Operation at the end of the week	1000	850	500	200	00

below:

The group replacement of 100 bulbs costs Rs. 1.00 and individual replacement cost Rs. 0.50 per bulb. Sugest a suitable replacement policy.

Objective Question

1. When money value changes with time @ 10% then p.w.f. for first year is

   a. 1 b. 0.909
   c. 0.852 d. 0.9

2. Which of the following maintanance policies is not used in old age of machine

   a. operate upto failure and do corrective maintenance.
   b. Reconditioning
   c. Replacement
   d. Scheduled preventive maintenance

3. When money value changes with time @ 20%, the discount for second year is

   a. 1 b. 0.833
   c. 0 d. 0.6955

4. A machine replaced with average running cost

   a. Is not equal to current running cost
   b. Till current period is greater than that of next period
   c. If current period is greater than that of next period
   d. If current period is less than that of next period

5. Group replacement policy is suitable for

   a. trucks
   b. infant machines
   c. Street light bulb
   d. New Car's

6. Replacement of an item will become necessary when

   a. Old item becomes too expensive to operate or maintain
   b. When your operator desire to work on a new machine
   c. When your oponent changes his machine in his unit
   d. When company has surplus funds to spend

7. In replacement analysis the maintenance cost is a function of

   a. time

b. function
c. initial investment
d. resale value

8. It is assume that maintenance cost mostly depends on
   a. Calender age
   b. Manufacturing dates
   c. Running age
   d. User age
9. If a machine becomes old, then the failure rate expected will be
   a. Constant
   b. Increasing
   c. Decreasing
   d. We cannot be said
10. Replacement is said to be necessary if
   a. Failure rate is increasing
   b. Failure cost is increasing
   c. Failure probabily is increasing
   d. Any of the above

Answer

1(b), 2(d), 3(a), 4(c), 5(d), 6(a), 7(a), 8(b), 9(c), 10(a)

Chapter 10

Queuing Theory

Course outline

10.1 Introduction

First time A.K. Erland, a Danish telephone Engineer, did original work on queuing theory. Erlang started his work in 1905 an attempt to determine the effects of fluctuating service demand (arrivals) on the utilization of automatic dialing equipment. In today's scenario a wide variety of seemingly diverse problems situations are recognized as being described by the general waiting line model.

In any queuing system, we have an input that arrives at some facility for service or processing and the time between the arrivals of individual's inputs at the service facility is commonly random in nature. For example, Doctor is a service facility and medical care is a service, ticket counter is a service facility and issue of ticket is service.

10.2 Queuing (Definition)

Queue or waiting lines stands for a number of customers waiting to be serviced. Queue does not include the customer being served. The process or system that performs the services to the customer is termed as service channel or service facility.

In general, we can say that a flow of customers from infinite or finite population towards the service facility forms a queue or waiting line on account of lack of capability to serve them all at time.

10.3 Queuing System

The formulation of queue is a common phenomenon which occurs whenever the current demand for a service exceeds the current capacity to provide that service. The queues of a people may be seen at a cinema ticket windows, bus stop, reservation office, counters of super market etc: The person waiting in a queue or receiving the service is a called the customer and the person by whom he is serviced is called a server.

Thus the whole queue system is described as follows:

(a) The input (or arrival pattern)

(b) Queue (or waiting line)

(c) The server discipline (or queue discipline)

(d) The service mechanism (or service pattern)

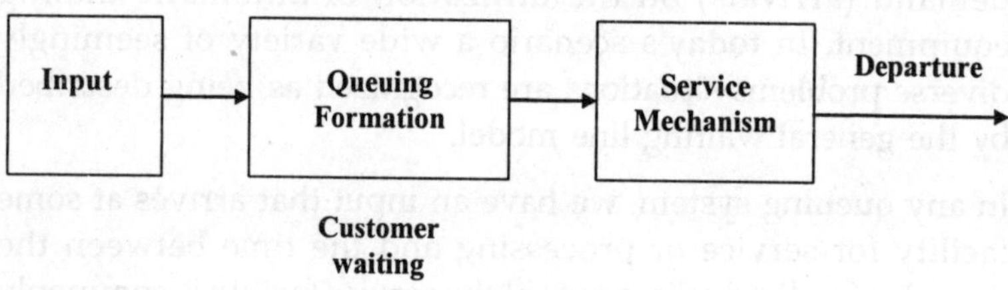

The basic Queuing system

(a) The input (or arrival pattern)

The input describes the pattern in which the customers arrive for service. Since the units for service in a random fashion therefore, their arrival pattern can be describe in terms of probabilities.

(b) Queue (or waiting line) formation

The units requiring service enter the queuing system on their arrival and join a "queue". A queue is called finite if the number of units in it is finite otherwise it is called infinite.

(c) The service discipline (or queue discipline):

The queue discipline is the manner in which the members in the queue are chosen for service. There are following queue disciplines:

(i) FCFS (First Come, First served):

According to this, the customers are served in the order of their arrival. This service discipline may be seen at a cinema ticket window, at a railway ticket window etc.

(ii) LCFS (Last come, First served):

According to this, the units (items) which come last are taken out (served) first.

(iii) SIRO (service in random order):

According to this, the customer are served in random order.

(iv) Service on some priority- procedure:

Some customers are served before the order without considering their order of arrival i.e. some customers are served on priority basis.

(d) The service mechanism (or service pattern):

The service mechanism refers to

(i) The pattern according to which the customers are served.

(ii) Facilities given to the customer.

(iii) Single channel (the customer are served by one counter only).

(iv) Multi-channel (here the customer are served by several counters).

1. Single line Facility

2. Single queue Parallel Facilities

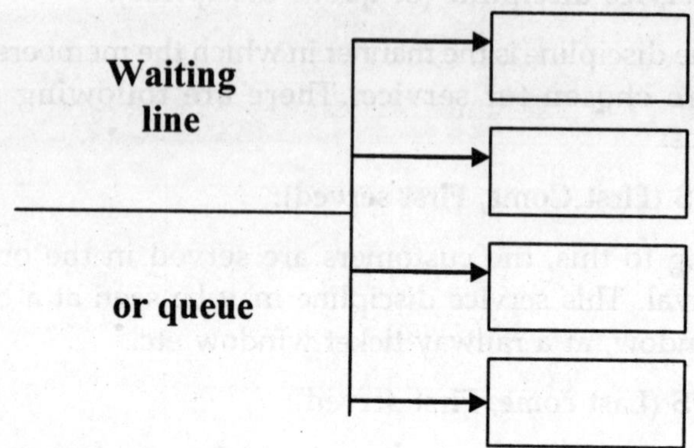

3. Multiple facilities

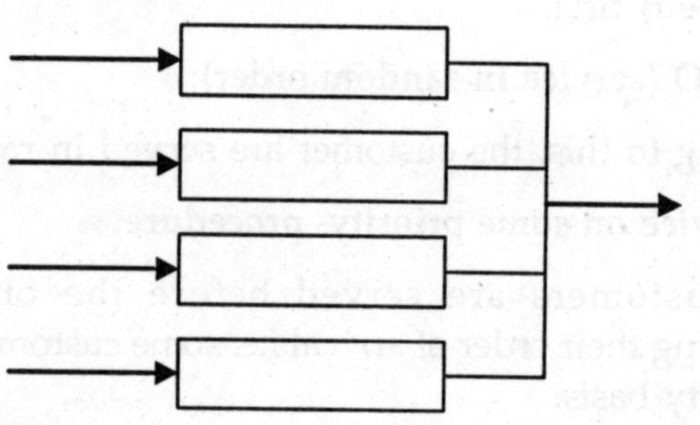

4. Series of facilities

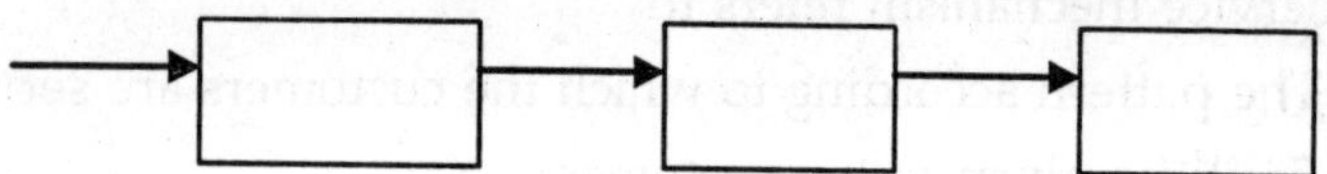

5. Combination of facilities

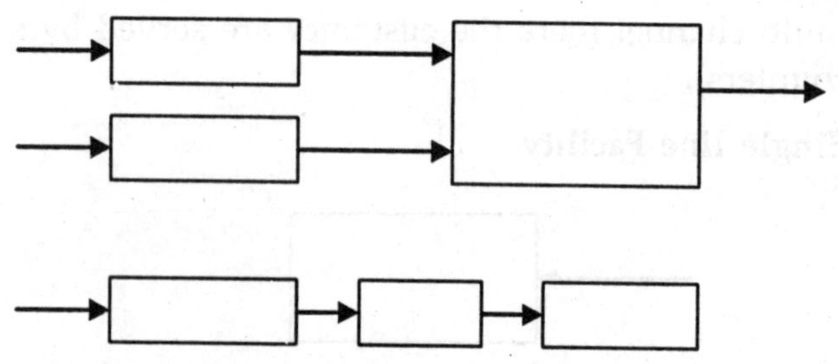

10.4 Queuing Situation

There are various queuing situation which are shows is every day life. In the queuing situation the customers are not only humans, but are non-human also.

Situation	Customers	Queue	Service Facility
Bank	Men and Women	Counter for cash withdrawl	ATM machines or counter clerk/tellers
Airlines	Men and Women	Ticket counter	Service/clerk/ca shier
Recuritment	Applicants	Arriving Candidate	Interviewers
Hospitals	Patient	Arriving Patient	Doctors

10.5 Queuing Model:

Kendall's notation for representing Queuing models

Generally, queuing model is represented by the following symbol form (a/b/c) :(d/e)

where

a = probability law for arrival time.

b = probability law according to which the customer are being served.

c = number of channels.

d = the maximum number allowed in the system (in service and waiting)

e = queue discipline.

Before dealing with carious models, we have to know certain symbols used.

	Poisson/ exponential	M
	Only mean and variance known	G
1. Arrival and service process	Erlang	Ek
	Constant	D
	Normal	N
2. Number of server	One	1
	More than one	k
3. Queue discipline	First come first serve	FCFS
	Priority	PRI
	Random Selection	SIRO
4. Maximum queue length	No limit	?
	Finite	n

Types of Queuing models

1. (M/M/1): (∞ / FCFS) Standard single server model
2. (M/M/k): (∞/FCFS) Standard Multiserver model
3. (M/Ek/1): (∞ / FCFS) Single Earlang service model
4. (M/G/1): (∞ / FCFS) Service time distribution unknown
5. (M/M/1): (∞ /PRI) Priority service, Single server
6. (M/M/1) :(n/FCFS) Finite queue, single server
7. (M/M/k): (n/FCFS) Finite queue, Multi server

1. (M/M/1): (∞ /FCFS) (Birth and death Model):

Let us assume that the arrival rate is random and hence described by Poisson distribution. It is denoted by (λ). Service rate is assumed to follow negative exponential distribution and is denoted by (μ).

(i) Average number of customers in the system

$$Ls = (\lambda) / (\mu - \lambda)$$

(ii) Expected queue length (Average number of customer in the system)

$$Lq = Ls - (\lambda / \mu) = (\lambda^2) / \{\mu(\mu - \lambda)\} = (\rho 2) / (1 - \rho)$$

(iii) Average waiting time $\omega = \dfrac{1}{\mu - \lambda}$

(iv) Average waiting time in queue

$$Wq = (\lambda) / \{\mu (\mu - \lambda)\}$$

(v) Average time in the system (Ws) = $\frac{1}{\mu - \lambda}$

(vi) Probability of an empty facility

$$P(0) = 1 - (\lambda / \mu)$$

(vii) Probability of system being busy

$$P(w) = 1 - P(0) = (\lambda / \mu)$$

(viii) Probability of being in the system longer than time t

$$P(T > t) = e^{-(\mu - \lambda) t}$$

(ix) Probability of customer not exceeding k in the system

$$P(n \geq k) = \rho^k \text{ and } (n > k) = \rho^{k+1}$$

(x) Probability of exactly N customers in the system $P(N) = \rho^n (1 - \rho)$

(xi) Traffic intensity (ρ) = (λ / μ)

Relationship between Ls, Lq, Ws, Wq

$Ls = (\lambda / \mu) / \{1 - (\lambda / \mu)\} = \lambda / (\mu / \lambda)$

$Ws = 1 / (\mu - \lambda)$

$Ls = \lambda Ws$

$Lq = \lambda Wq$

and $Wq = Ws - (1/\mu)$

$Lq = Ls - (\lambda/\mu)$

Example 1. A departmental store has a single cashier. During the rush hours, customers arrive at the rate of 20 customers per hour. The average number of customer that can be processed by the cashier is 24 per hour. Assume that the conditions for the use of single - channel queuing model apply what is the

(a) Probability the cashier is idle

(b) Average time of customers in the queue

(c) Average number of customers spends in the system

(d) Average time customer spends in the queue waiting for service

Solution:

Mean arrival rate (λ) = 20 customer per hour

Mean service rate (μ) = 24 customer per hour

hence

(a) Probability that the cashier is idle = P (0)

$= 1 - (\lambda / \mu)$

$= 1 - (20/24) = (4/24) = (1/6) = 0.167$

(b) Average number of customers in the queuing system (Ls)

$= (\lambda) / (\mu - \lambda)$

$= 20 / (24-20) = 20/4 = 5$ customers

(c) Expected average waiting time of customer in the system (Ws)

$= 1 / (\mu - \lambda)$

$= 1 / (24-20)$

$= 1/ 4$ hrs

(d) Average number of customer in the queue (Lq) = Ls - (λ / μ)

$= (20 / 24) * \{ 20 / (20 - 24)\}$

$= (5/ 6) \times (5) = 25 / 6 = 4\frac{1}{6}$ customers

(e) Average time a customer spend in the queue before service

$Wq = (\lambda) / \{\mu (\mu - \lambda)\}$

$= 20 / \{ 24 (24- 20)\}$

$= 5/ (6 * 4) = 5/ 24$ hrs

= 12.5 minutes

Example 2. A T.V. repairman finds that the time spent on his job has an exponential distribution with mean 30 minutes. If he repairs set in order in which they come and if the arrival sets is approximately Poisson with an average rate 10 per 8 hrs day, what is his expected idle time each day? How many jobs are ahead of the set just brought in ?

Solution:

Here $\lambda = 1/30$, $\mu = 10 / (8 \times 60) = 1/48$

Expected number of jobs is

$Ls = (\lambda) / (\mu - \lambda)$

$= (1/48) / \{(1/30)-(1/48)\} = 30/18=10/6=5/3 = 1.67$

The probability that the repairman is busy = $P(w)= (\lambda/\mu)$

The number of hours for which the repairman is busy in 8 hrs day = $8 (\lambda/\mu)$

$= 8 \times (\lambda / \mu)$

$= 8 \times (30 / 48) = 5$ hrs

Therefore, the time for which the repairman's idle in an 8 hrs day = (8-5)=3 hrs

Example 3: At a service counter of fast food joint, the customers arrive at the average intervals of six minutes whereas the counter clerk takes on an average 5 min. for preparation of bill and delivery of the items.

(a) Counter utilization level.

(b) Average waiting time of in the line.

(c) Average number of customer in the service counter area.

(d) Average number of customer in the line.

(e) Probability that of customer clerk is idle.

(f) Probability of finding the clerk is busy.

(g) Chances that customer is required to wait more than 30 minutes in the system.

(h) Probability of having four customers in the system.

(i) Probability of finding more than 3 customers in the system.

Solution:

Given that

If customer arrive at an average interval of six minutes, the average arrival rate

$\lambda = 60/6 = 10$ customer per hour

when customers are served by the clerk every 5 minutes on the average, the expected service rate

$\mu = 60/5 = 12$ customer per hour

(a) Counter utilization level = traffic intensity = λ / μ

$= 10/12 = 0.833$

(b) Average waiting time of the customers at the fast food joint

$Ws = 1 / (\mu - \lambda)$

$= 1/(12-10)$

$= 1/2$ hrs = 30 minutes

(c) Expected average waiting time in the line

$Wq = (\lambda) / \{\mu (\mu - \lambda)\}$

$= (10/12) (1/ 12-10) = 5 /12$ hrs = 25 minutes

(d) Average number of customers in service counter area.

$Ls = (\lambda) / (\mu - \lambda)$

$= 10 / (12 - 10) = 5$ customers

(e) Average number of customers in the line

$(Lq) = Ls - (\lambda / \mu)$

$= (10 /12) (10 / 12-10)$

=26 /6 = 4 customers

(f) Probability that the counter is idle

$P(0) = (1 - \lambda / \mu)$

$= (1 - 10/12)$

$= 1/6$

$= 0.167$

(g) Probability of finding the clerk busy

$P(w) = 1 - P(0) = 1 - 0.167 = 0.833$

(h) Chances that customer waits more than 30 minutes in the system

$P(T>t) = e^{-(\mu - \lambda)t} = e^{-(12-10)/2} = e^{-1}$

$= 0.368$

(i) Probability of having 4 customers in the system

$P(4) = \rho^n (1-\rho)$

$= (\lambda/\mu)^4 (1 - \lambda/\mu)$

$= (0.833)(1-0.833) = 0.0804$

(j) Probability of finding more than 5 customers in the system $P(k > 3) = \rho^{k+1}$

$= (0.833)$

$= 0.482$

2. (M/M/1) : (N/FCFS) :

In this model, the capacity of the system is limited (finite). Say N obviously, the number of arrivals will not exceed the number N in any case.

1. $P_0 = (1 - \rho) / (1 - \rho^{N+1})$
2. $P_0 = \{(1 - \rho)/(1-\rho^{N+1})\} \rho^n$ for n = 0, 1, 2......N
3. $Lq = \lambda/\mu$

N

4. $Ls = \rho^0 \Sigma n \rho^n$
   $n=0$
5. $Lq = Ls - (\lambda/\mu)$
6. $Ws = Ls / \lambda$
7. $Wq = Lq / \lambda$

Example 1: In a railway marshalling yard, goods train arrives at the rate of 30 trains per day. Assume that the inter arrival time follows an exponential distribution and the service time is also to be assumed as exponential with mean of 36 minutes. Calculate

(a) The probability that the yard is empty.

(b) The average queue length assuming that the line capacity of the yard is 9 trains.

Solution: Given time

$\lambda = 30 / (60*24) = 1/48$, $\mu = 1/16$ train per minute

$\rho = (\lambda/\mu) = 36/48 = 0.75$

The probability that the queue is empty is given by $P_0 = (1 - \lambda) / (1 - \rho^{N+1})$

$= (1\text{-} 0.75) / \{1 - (0.75)^{10}\}$

$= 0.25 / 0.90 = 0.28$

(2) Average queue length is given by $Ls = \rho^o \times \left(\sum_{n=0}^{9} n \rho^n \right)$

$= (0.28) \times \left(\sum_{n=0}^{9} (0.75)^n \right) = 0.28 \times 9.58 = 3$ trains

Example. 2 Assuming for a period of 2 hrs in a day (8-10 am) trains arrive at the yard every 20 minutes, then calculate for this period.

(i) The probability that the yard is empty.

(ii) Average queue length assuming that the capacity of the yard is 4 trains only.

Solution: Given that

$\rho = 36 / 20 = 1.8$, $N = 4$

(i) $P_0 = (\rho - 1) / (\rho^5 - 1) = 0.4$

(ii) Average queue size$= P_0 \times \left(\sum_{n=0}^{4} n \rho^n \right)$

$= 0.04 (\rho + 2\rho^2 + 3\rho^3 + 4\rho^4)$

$= 2.9 = 3$ trains

10.6 Practice Problem:

1. What is queuing theory? What are its limitations?
2. Define a queue with an example. What are the types of queues?
3. What are the characteristics of queuing system?
4. Write short note on queuing theory.
5. What is a "Queuing Model" ? What are its objectives?
6. Give the basic structure of (M/M/1) queuing model?
7. Write important assumptions of queuing models.
8. Explain following terms:
   a. Queue length
   b. Traffic intensity
   c. Waiting Time
   d. Arrival Rate
   e. Service Rate
9. Explain the single channel and multi-channel queuing models.
10. What is the waiting line problem? Give three business applications of waiting line theory.
11. Write short note on Birth and death Process.
12. Describe the different types of costs involved in a queuing

system.

13. Draw a diagram showing the physical layout of a queuing system with multi-server, multi-channel service facility.
14. People arrive at a theater ticket center in a Poisson distributed arrival rate of 25 per hour. Service time is constant at 2 minutes. Calculate
    a. The mean number in the waiting line.
    b. The mean waiting time.
    c. Utilization factor

[Ans. (i) 4 people (ii) 10 Minutes (iii) p =0.833]

15. Car arrive at a petrol pump with exponential inter arrival time having mean 1/2 minute. The attendant takes on an average of 1/5 minute per car to supply petrol.

    The service time is exponentially distributed. Determine
    a. The average number of cars waiting to be served.
    b. The average number of cars in the queue.
    c. The proportion of time for which the pump attendant is idle.

[Ans. (i) 2 cars (ii) 4/3 cars (iii) 0.34]

16. In a railway marshalling yard, goods train arrives at the rate of 30 trains per day. Assume that the inter arrival time follows an exponential distributed and the service time is also to be assumed as exponential with mean 36 minutes. Calculate
    a. The probability that the yard is empty.
    b. The average queue length assuming that the line capacity of the yard is 9 trains.

[Ans.(i) 0.28 (ii) 3 trains]

17. A two channel waiting line with Poisson arrival has a mean arrival rate of 50 per hour and exponential service with a mean service rate of 75 per hour for each channel. Find
    a. The probability of an empty system.
    b. The probability that an arrival in the system will have to wait.

[Ans.(i) 0.83 (ii) 0.167]

18. There are two clerks in a university to receive dues from the students. If the service time for each student is exponential with mean 4 minutes and if the boys arrive in a Poisson fashion at the counter at the rate 10 per hour. Determine
    a. The probability of having to wait for service.
    b. The expected percentage of idle time for each clerk?

[Ans. (i) 0.167 (ii) 0.67]

Objective Problem

1. The expediting or follow up function in production control is an example of
   (a) LIFO
   (b) SIRO
   (c) FIFO
   (d) Preemptive
2. In (M/M/1) : (N/FIFO) the following does not apply
   (a) Poisson arrival (b) Limited service
   (c) Exponential service (d) Single service
3. In queue designation (a/b/c) : (d/e) , what does c represent?
   (a) Arrival Pattern
   (b) Service pattern
   (c) Number of service channels
   (d) Capacity of the system
4. Queuing models measures the effect of :
   (a) Random arrivals
   (b) Random service
   (c) Effect of uncertainty on the behavior of the queuing system
   (d) Length of queue
5. Traffic intensity is given by:
   (a) Mean arrival rate / mean service rate
   (b) $\lambda \times \mu$
   (c) μ / λ

(d) Number present in the queue/ Number served.

6. For a simple queue (M/M/1) , $\rho = \lambda / \mu$ is known as :
   (a) Poisson busy period
   (b) Random factor
   (c) Traffic intensity
   (d) Exponential service factor

7. SIRO discipline is generally found in:
   (a) Loading and unloading
   (b) Office filing
   (c) Lottery draw
   (d) Trains arrivals at platform

8. Office filing system follows:
   (a) LIFO
   (b) FIFO
   (c) SIRO
   (d) SBP

9. In (M/M/1) : (8 /FIFO) model , the length of the system Ls is given by :
   (a) $p^2 / 1/p$
   (b) $p/ (1 - \lambda)$
   (c) $\lambda^2 / (\mu - \lambda)$
   (d) $\lambda^2 / \mu (\mu - \lambda)$

10. In (M/ M/ 1) : (8/FIFO) model, $1/ (\mu - \lambda)$ represents:
   (a) Ls, Length of the system
   (b) Lq Length of the queue
   (c) Wq waiting time in queue
   (d) Ws waiting time in system

[Ans. 1 (d) 2 (d) 3 (a) 4 (c) 5 (a) 6 (c) 7 (c) 8 (a) 9 (b) 10 (c)]

Chapter 11

Decision Making Environment

Course Outline

11.1 Introduction

Decision making is very important part of human life. Every human being has to take decision in every day. The success of any organization, company, industry and life of human totally depend on the decision making. So it is major role of a manager too. The decisions taken by a manager have a various impact on business. Thus, we can say that the decision making is an integral part of management for planning, organizing, evaluating and controlling process. The decision makers have various strategies but he has to select best of them. It is not only important for the manager but also important for the employers, employee, creditors, stock holders, unions, government etc.

In fact the decision should be made whenever the organization or an individual faces problem of decision making or dissatisfied with the existing decisions. Then it becomes necessary to take a rational decision to improve the situation.

Thus we can say that the decision making is the first step of the organization activity because right decision gives the salutary effect and the wrong one may prove to be disastrous.

11.2 Decision theory

Decision theory provides a method for taking decision when the situations are not fully deterministic. Decision maker has to apply various methods for solving the decision problems. So decision theory identifies the best alternative or course of action for solving the problems. It is a framework for better understanding the situation and evaluating the system through the application of scientific method to solve the problems.

11.3 Types of Decision

In general, decision can be classified into three categories:

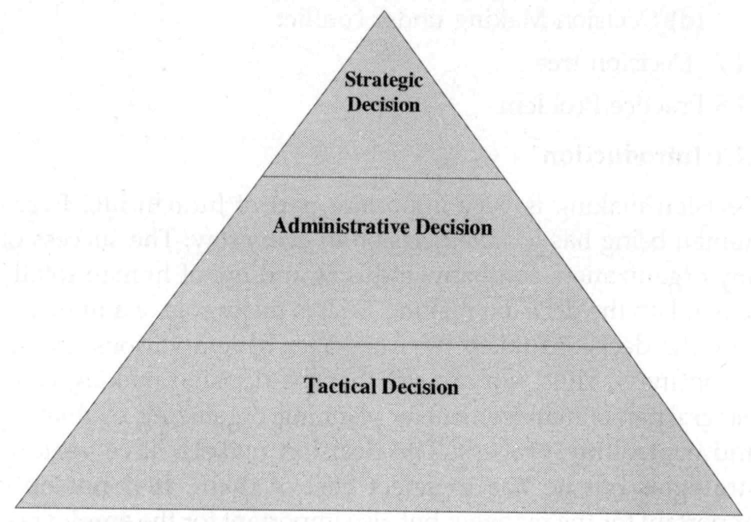

1. Strategic Decision :-

Strategic decision is for top level management. It is related to external environment of the organization. For example, the decision of selection of product mix which a firm will produce etc are comes in this category.

2. **Administrative Decision:-**

It is also called the managerial decision. This is concerned with the structuring and acquisition of the organization resources so as to optimize the performance of the organization.

For example: Selection of distribution channels etc.

3. **Tactical Decision:-**

It is also called the operating decision. This is concerned with day –to –day operations of the organization. For example, the decision related to the daily wages of the labour.

11.4 Component of Decision Making

There are various component of decision making which is given below:

1. **The decision maker: -** The Decision maker is a person who takes the decision. He has the various alternatives to select best of them.
2. **Objective: -** The decision maker has some desire. He has to achieve these desired which is called objective.
3. **Event: -** Events are the occurrences which affect the achievement of the objective.
4. **The Environment: -** The decision maker has the problem in an environment.
5. **Alternative course of action: -** A problem always involved a question: what to do? This question becomes a problem only when alternative course of action are available.
6. **Payoff table: -** The payoff can be interpreted as the outcome in quantitative form if the decision maker adopts a particular strategy under a particular state of nature.
7. **Opportunity loss table:-** An opportunity loss is the loss incurred because of failure to take the best possible action.

11.5 Process of Decision Making

The decision making process is divided into four stages. These are following:

Stage 1. Define the problem

In the first stage, the decision maker has to define the problem for which decision made.

Stage 2. Search for alternatives

In this stage the decision maker search the alternatives for solving the problem. There are various alternative for solving the problem.

Stage 3. Evaluate for alternatives

In this stage the decision maker has to evaluate various alternatives and set the priorities for each alternative.

Stage 4. Select an alternative

In this stage the decision maker has to chosen the best alternatives which meet its objective or we can say that which gives best outcomes or which is the best decision.

11.6 Decision Making Environment

Every decision depends upon the two factors first is the course of action and second is the decision environment. Basically, there are four different states of decision environments, certainty, uncertainty, risk and conflict.

1. Decision making under certainty:-

It is a simple form of decision making. There is one state of nature of each alternatives course of action and there is accurate knowledge about the outcomes of each alternative. In the situation where decision making under certainty include the allocation of resources to various product line. The alternatives are evaluated in terms of cost of each alternative. Hence it is not real life situation. For example, a new car buying, the decision maker would have certainty about the price and specification of each car therefore the decision maker is easy to take the decision. In this situation the decision maker may use various techniques like linear programming, transportation, assignment model and EOQ model etc.

2. Decision making under uncertainty:-

In this situation decision making process is more complicated. Since the data or information is incomplete or we can say that there is no idea or knowledge about the probabilities of the various state of nature and the expected value of various alternatives can not be calculated. For example, the marketing of new product in such situation there is no single best criterion of selecting a strategy.

There are number of criterion available for making decision under uncertainty.

a) The Maximax criterion

The term **Maximax** means **"Maximum of the maximums"**. Application of the Maximax criteria requires a table of gains.

Eg. Suppose for each states of nature there are three Decisions given in the following matrix:

States of Nature	Decisions			Maximum of each row
	A_1	A_2	A_3	
S_1	200	160	80	200
S_2	140	170	160	170
S_3	120	150	180	180
Maximax	Maximum (Maximum of each row)			200

Conclusion: In Maximax criterion the decision - maker should take decision A_1.

b) The Minimax criterion

Minimax is just opposites of Maximax. The term Minimax means **"Minimum of the Maximum"**. The Minimax rule minimize the Maximum possible loss of each course of action . It is for the risk avoider decision maker. Application of the Minimax criteria requires a table of losses.

Eg. Find out the Minimax decision criterion for following matrix:

States of Nature	Decision			Maximum of each row
	A_1	A_2	A_3	
S_1	1	5	11	11
S_2	4	1	7	7
S_3	19	14	1	19
Minimax	Minimum (Maximum of each row)			7

Conclusion: In Minimax criterion the decision-maker should take action A_3.

c) The Laplace criterion:

In this method the decision maker has no information about the probability of occurrence of various events, the decision maker has to make a simple assumption that each probability is equally likely. The act having maximum expected payoff is selected.

Events	Action			Assume (Probability)
	A_1	A_2	A_3	
E_1	25	27	30	1/3
E_2	30	20	35	1/3
E_3	35	25	27	1/3

Example:

$A_1 \rightarrow (25\times1/3) + (30\times1/3) + (35\times1/3) = 30$

$A_2 \rightarrow (27\times1/3) + (20\times1/3) + (25\times1/3) = 24$

$A_3 \rightarrow (30\times1/3) + (35\times1/3) + (27\times1/3) = 30.67$

Since A_3 has maximum expected payoff, A_3 is the optimal act.

d) The Hurwicz criterion:

It is the combination of maximum criterion and minimum criterion. In this method, the decision maker's degree of optimism is represented by α, varies 0 and 1. When $\alpha = 0$, there is total pessimism and when $\alpha = 1$, there is total optimism.

$D_i = \alpha Mi + (1 - \alpha) m_i$

Where M_i is the maximum payoff of ith decision.

m_i is the minimum payoff of ith decision.

Example.

Events	Act			
	A_1	A_2	A_3	**$\alpha = \alpha 6$, $D_i = \alpha Mi + (1- \alpha)$**
E_1	25	17	30	D_1=(0.6*35)+(1-0.6)20=29
E_2	30	20	35	D_2=(0.6*25)+(1-0.6)17=21.8
E_3	35	25	27	D_3=(0.6*35)+(1-0.6)27=31.8

Since D_3 is maximum , select the act A_3.

C. Decision making under risk:-

In decision making under condition of risk, the decision maker has sufficient information to assign probabilities to each of the following criterion but in the case of decision making under condition of uncertainty the decision-maker does not have sufficient information to assign probability to different states of nature.

There are following methods which are used in decision making under risk.

a) EMV (Expected Monetary Value)

In this method, the probability of each states of nature is to be given. And we have to calculate the expected gain of each course of action.

Example:

Let us assume that the states of nature be S_1 and S_2 , the alternative strategies be A_1 and A_2 and the probability for the each states of nature be 0.6 and 0.4 respectively.

	A_1	A_2	**Probability**
S_1	25	15	0.6
S_2	30	25	0.4
EMV	(25×0.6)+(30×0.4)=27	(15×0.6)+(25×0.4)=19	
	Since the EMV for A_1 is greater. Thus the decision maker will choose the strategy A_1.		

Since the EMV for A_1 is greater. Thus the decision maker will choose the strategy A_1.

b) EOL (Expected Opportunity Loss)

Opportunity loss is the difference between the greater payoff and the actual payoff. The probability of each states of nature will be available, and the EOL of each strategy has to calculate. The strategy which has minimum expected opportunity Loss (EOL) is chosen.

Example:

Let us consider that the states of nature be S_1 and S_2 and S_3 and the alternative strategies be A_1 A_2 and A_3 and the probabilities for corresponding strategies be 0.3, 0.3 and 0.4 respectively.

	A_1	A_2	A_3
Prob.	0.3	0.3	0.4
S_1	15	25	45
S_2	20	55	65
S_3	25	40	70

Opportunity Loss Table

	A_1	A_2	A_3
Prob.	0.3	55-0.3	700.4
S_1	25-15	55-25	70-45
S_2	25-20	55-55	70-65
S_3	25-25	55-40	70-70

Now

	A_1	A_2	A_3
Prob.	0.3	0.3	0.4
S_1	10	30	25
S_2	5	0	5
S_3	0	15	0

Hence EOL $(S_1) = 0.3 \times 10 + 0.3 \times 30 + 0.4 \times 25 = 13$

EOL $(S_2) = 0.3 \times 5 + 0.3 \times 0 + 0.4 \times 5 = 3.5$

EOL $(S_3) = 0.3 \times 0 + 0.3 \times 15 + 0.4 \times 0 = 4.5$

The strategy S_1 will be selected due to maximum EOL for S_1 is equal to 13

c) EVPI (Expected Value of Perfect Information):

The expected value with perfect information (EVPI) is the expected result with perfect information minus the highest EMV. The probability of each states of nature is known.

Therefore

EVPI= Total Expected result – Max. EMV

Example:

Let us assume that the states of nature be S_1, S_2, and S_3, the alternative strategies be A_1, A_2 and A_3 and the probability is 0.5 , 0.4 , and 0.1.

	A_1	A_2	A_3	Probability
S_1	25	20	17	0.5
S_2	15	30	15	0.4
S_3	35	25	30	0.1
EMV	(25×0.5) + (15×0.4) + (35×0.1) = 22.0	(20×0.5) + (30×0.4) + (25×0.1) =24.5	(17×0.5) + (15×0.4) + (30×0.1) = 17.5	
	The highest EMV is 24.5.			

	Max. profit of each state	Probability	Expected result= (probability×profit)
S	25	0.5	12.5
S	30	0.4	12
S	35	0.1	3.5
	Expected result with perfect information		28

Now Expected result with perfect information is

EVPI = (Total Expected Result) – (Maximum EMV)

= 28-24.5

= 3.5

4. Decision making under conflict:-

When two or more person wants to get one thing then conflict arises. Under this situation the decision is called decision making under conflict. Game theory deals with those problems in which the decision maker is in conflict or competition with his opponents. The courses of action available to the opponent become the states of nature that face the decision maker. In this situation the opponent try to damage the decision maker as much as possible, and will try to minimize his maximum losses.

11.7 Decision Tree

Decision tree is a graphical representation of the decision process indicating decision alternatives, states of nature, probabilities attached to the states of nature and profits and losses associated with it. It consists of nodes and branches. The following symbols are used-

1. Decision Node ☐

2. State of nature ○

3. Branches ╲

Different course of action (or strategies) emerge out of the nodes as main branches of the decision tree. At the end of each decision branch, there is a node representing state of nature out of which sub-branches comeout representing change events. The payoff from those alternatives and their probability of occurrence are shown along side of these branches.

"Decision tree" one of the method for solving complex decision problem. A decision tree is generally useful for multistage situation which involve a series of decisions each depend upon the preceding one. Thus the decision problem can be represented graphically with the help of decision tree, such graphical representation facilitates the decision making p[rocess.

Example 1. A manufacturing company has to option for increasing the profit the first option is to launch the new product and the second option is to modify the existing product. The production of a new product can be justified on the grounds that if the demand increases otherwise it may be advisable modify the existing product for increasing demand.

Solution.

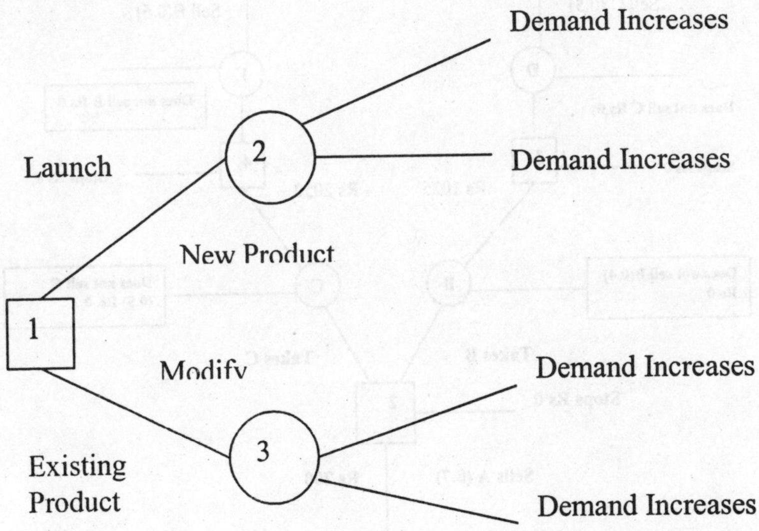

Example.2 A client has an estate agent to sell three properties A,B and C for him and agrees to pay him 5% commission on each sale. He specifies certain conditions. The estate agent must sell property A first and this he must do within 60 days. If and when A is sold the agent receive 5% commission on that sale.He can the back out at this stage or nominate and try to sell one if the remaining two properties within 60 days. If he does not successed in selling the nominated property in that period, he is not given opportunity to sell the property on the same conditions. The price, selling costs (incurred by the estate agent whenever a sale is made) and the estate agents estimated probability of making a sale are given below:

Property	Price of Property	Selling Costs	Prob. Of sales
A	12000	400	0.7
B	25000	225	0.6
C	50000	450	0.5

Draw up an appropriate decision tree for the estate agent.

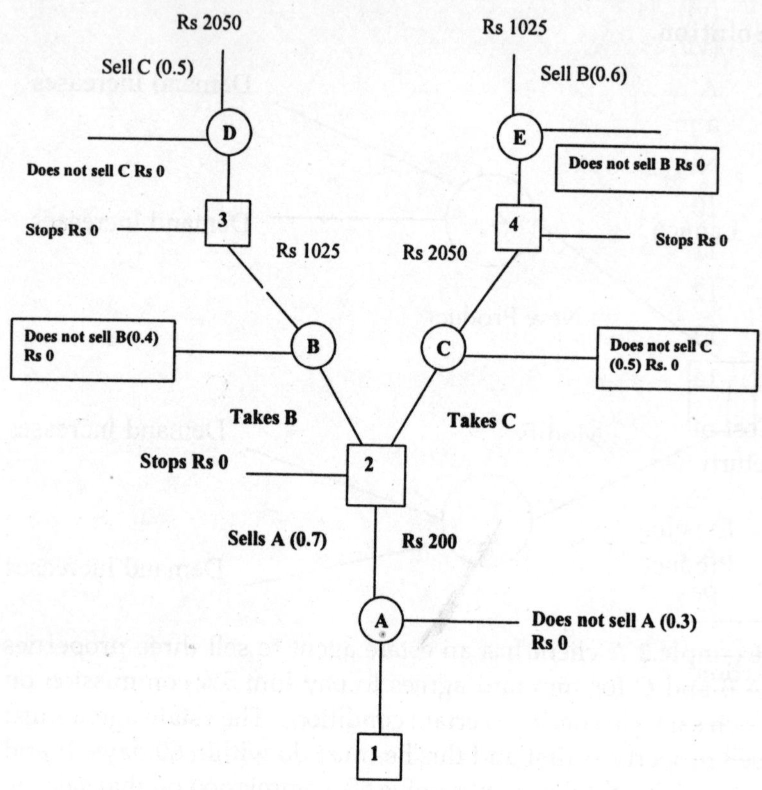

11.8 Practice Problem

1. What do you mean by decision theory?
2. Explain the decision making situation?
3. What are the components of decision making?
4. What do you mean by "Decision Tree"?
5. Write short notes on following.

(i) EMV
(ii) EOL
(iii) EVPI
(iv) Laplace criterion
(v) The Maximini decision criterion(criterion of pessimism)
(vi) The Maximax decision criterion (criterion of optimism)
(vii) Hurwichz criterion

6. A newspaper boy has the following probability of selling a magazine.

No. of copies	Probability
10	0.10
11	0.15
12	0.20
13	0.25
14	0.30

Cost of a copy is 30 paise and sale price is 50 paise. He can not return unsold copies. How many copies he should order?

[Ans. No. of copies to be ordered =12]

7. A decision problem has been expressed in the following pay-off table.

	Outcome		
Action	I	II	III
A	10	20	26
B	30	30	60
C	40	30	20

(a) What is minimum pay-off?
(b) What is the minimum opportunity loss function?

8. A farmer wants to plan which of the three crops he should plant on his 100 acre form. The profit of each crop depends upon the rain fall during the growing season. The rainfall could be high, medium and low. The estimated profit of the former for each of the crops is as shown in the table.

Estimated conditional Profit			
Rainfall	Crop A	Crop B	Crop C
High	6000	3000	7000
Medium	4000	4500	4000
Low	2000	5000	5000

The farmer decides to plant only one crop, which would be his best crop use the following criterion.

(a) Maximum

(b) Maximin

(c) Laplace

(d) Minimax Regret

9. The research department of Hindustan lever has recommended to the marketing department to launch a shampoo of three different type. The marketing manager has to decide one of the types of shampoo to be launched under the following estimated payoffs.

Estimated level of sales			
Types of shampoo	15000	10000	5000
Egg. Shampoo	30	10	10
Clinic Shampoo	40	15	5
Delux Shampoo	55	20	3

What will be the marketing managing decision of (i) Maximax (ii) Minimax (iii) Maximax (iv) Laplace (v) EOL (vi) EMV (vii) EVPI

10 . The estimated sales of proposed types on perfumes are as under:

Estimated level of sales			
Types of perfume	Rs. 20000	Rs. 10000	Rs.20000
A	25	15	10
B	40	20	5
C	60	25	3

(a) For each of the following decision. State the optical action and specify the value leading to its selection (i) Maximin (ii) Maximax (iii) Laplace (iv) Minimax Regret (v) EOL (vi) EMV (vii) EVPI

(b) What will be the optimal act if payoff entries represent the costs instead of sales?

11. Consider the following pay-off (profit) matrix.

	Q1	Q2	Q3	Q4
a1	5	10	18	25
a2	8	7	8	23
a3	21	18	12	21
a4	30	22	19	15

Solve the using Hurwicz criterion with $\alpha = 0.73$

12. The daily demand for bread in a grocery store can be one of the value out of 200, 260 or 300 loves with probability of 0.5, 0.3 and 0.2. the owner of the store wants to store one of these numbers. Assuming that the bread costs Rs. 10 and is sold for Rs.15; find the optimum stock level using decision tree representation.

Objective Question

1. The maximum decision criterion stands for
   (a) Maximum of Minimum
   (b) Minimum of Maximum
   (c) Maximum of Maximum
   (d) Minimum of Minimum
2. The optimism decision criterion stands for
   (a) Maximum decision criterion
   (b) Minimum decision criterion
   (c) Minimum decision criterion
   (d) Maximum decision criterion
3. The difference between the greater pay off and the actual pay off is known as
   (a) Opportunity profit
   (b) Opportunity table
   (c) Opportunity loss
   (d) Opportunity situations

4. For decision problems under risk, the most popular methods used are
   (a) Laplace, Hurwicz
   (b) EMV, Maximin
   (c) Maximin, Minimax
   (d) EMV, EOL
5. ________ is one of the devices of representing diagrammatic presentation of sequential and multi dimensional aspects of a particular decision problem for systemic analysis and evaluation
   (a) Flowchart
   (b) Decision tree
   (c) Bar charts
   (d) Pie charts
6. When a new product introduced in a market this situation come under:
   (a) Decision making under uncertainity
   (b) Decision making under conflict
   (c) Decision making under risk
   (d) Decision making under certainity
7. When the outcome of the decision is known this is called
   (a) Decision making under conflict
   (b) Decision making under risk
   (c) Decision making under certainity
   (d) Decision making under uncertainity
8. The theory of game is the example of
   (a) Decision making under certainity
   (b) Decision making under risk
   (c) Decision making under uncertainity
   (d) Decision making under conflict
9. EMV stands for
   (a) Expected Monetary Value
   (b) Expected Measurement Value
   (c) Expected Moving Value
   (d) Excess Money Value

10. EVPI stands for
    (a) Expected Value with Perfect Information
    (b) Expected Volume with Profit Initiation
    (c) Expected Value with Profit Index
    (d) Excess Value with Profit Index.

[Ans 1(a), 2 (a), 3(c), 4(d), 5(b), 6(a), 7(c), 8(d), 9(a) 10(a)]

Chapter 12

Project Management

Course outline

12.1 Introduction

The historical development of project is as old as human beings. It is started with the early civilization such as shown in ancient writings of many countries. A project is a non-routine activity that must be completed with a definite amount of resources and within definite time limit.

It may be defined as, "a non-routine activities with complex in nature and may be completed with a set amount of resources and within a set time limit."

12.2 Project Management

Project Management is related with planning, scheduling, controlling the activities which is not in routine nature and that must be completed to obtain the pre-determine objectives of the project. or It is an investment made for a package of inter-related time bound activities.

Each and every project has two phase as

(i) Preparation and construction.

(ii) Its process and operation.

Project planning is done in advance which deals with various tasks, operation or activities that must be performed to achieve the project objectives.

The project has to be operated within certain rules and regulations with restrictions. A project needs resources or input for implementation to get desired output.

12.3 Project cycle

In a project cycle following are the basic element.

(i) Operation

(ii) Resources

(iii) Restraints

(i) Operations:- It is an important aspect that are related with the activities or jobs. The activities should be identified and arrange in a sequence to get the project objectives.

(ii) Resources:- Resources are an important tools which can be classified under manpower, money, material, machine and time. The time is related with the expected duration of the resources use.

(iii) Restraints:- It refers externally imposed conditions such as supply of materials, machines.

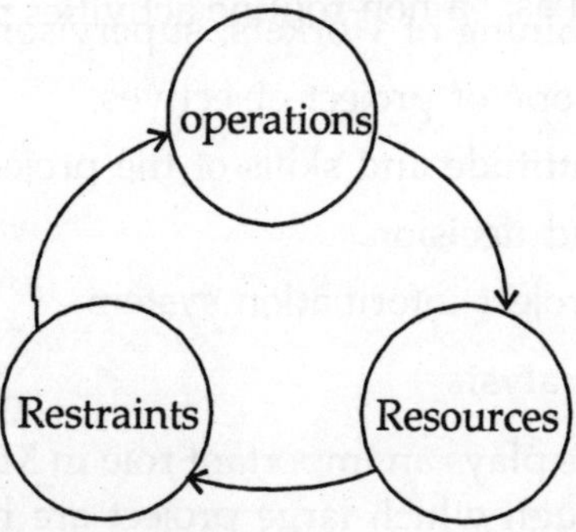

Causes of Delay in Project:

There are two causes of delay in project.

(1) External causes of delay (Or uncontrollable factor for delay):-There may be delay in project due to following external causes.

(i) Socio-Political

(ii) Economic

(iii) Technological

(iv) Macro and micro global reasons

Government policies, import regulations, resources constraints, political situation and inflation are the uncontrollable factors which produce delay in project.

(2) Internal causes of dealy (or controllable factor for delay): It is related to the programme, policies and planning of the company or organization.

These are as follows:-

(i) Delays in receiving information on change.

(ii) Frequent change in design and technology.

(iii) Weak monitoring and control.

(iv) Allowing project duration to expand.

Factors helping in completion of the project without delay:-

(i) Sound monitoring.

(ii) Selection of appropriate feasible technology.

(iii) Adequate training of workers, supervisors involved.

(iv) Clarity of scope of project objectives.

(v) Innovative attitude and skills of the project team.

(vi) Decentralized decision.

(vii) Adequate project information system.

12.4 Network Analysis

Network Analysis plays an important role in Management. It is a technique through which large project are broken down to individuals jobs or events and arranged in a logical network. It helps in identifying those jobs or events which control the completion of the project and also compute the optimum time of completion of project with minimum cost. We can say that it is a management tool for decision making. .

PERT and CPM are two techniques which are accepted now. These two techniques define and coordinate various activities of a project and successfully accomplish the objective on time.

12.5 Objective of Network Analysis

1. Optimum utilization of available resources.
2. To complete the project within the given period.
3. Optimization of costs and time required for the completion of the project.
4. To reduced the set up costs.
5. To reduced the indirect cost.

12.6 Advantages of Network Analysis

1. It is helpful for the completion of the optimum project duration.
2. It is a technique by which we can reduce the cost of the project.
3. It is important tool for planning, scheduling and control of the project.
4. It provides better analysis and logical thinking.
5. It identifies critical activities and provides greater attention.

6. It also identifies the critical path.
7. It provides up-to-date information on the progress of the projects.
8. It identifies earliest time and latest time for each activity.
9. It is very simple and easy to apply.
10. It also helps to optimize the resources.

12.7 Limitation of Network Analysis

1. Construction of Network for complex project is complicated and time consuming.
2. Estimation of accurate and reliable time of various activities is difficult job.
3. It becomes expensive due to large number of activities.
4. Time cost tradeoff procedure in many situations is complicated.

12.8 Application of Network Analysis

1. Constructions of buildings, dams, bridges, etc.
2. Manufacturing of ships, aeroplanes etc.
3. Advertising and sales promotion strategies.
4. Inventory control strategies.
5. Organization of conferences, public works.
6. Defense operation.
7. Research and development etc.

12.9 Basic Terms

There are the following terms which are use for understanding the Network Analysis

(i) Activity
(ii) Event
(iii) Path
(iv) Predecessor activity
(v) Successor activity

(vi) Dummy activity
(vii) Network diagram
(viii) Looping
(ix) Dangling

(i) Activity

In network Analysis activity is represented by an arrow, the tail of the arrow represent start and the head of the arrow represent the finish of the task. The length, shape and direction of the arrow have no relation to the size of the activity.

(ii) Event

An event represent the time at which an activity starts and finishes. It is represented by circle i.e. called node. The beginning time of an activity is Tail event and finishing time of an activity is head event.

(iii) Path

Path is a chain of activity which is connected by one event to another event.

(iv) Predecessor Activity

The activity which must be completed immediately before the start of another activity.

(v) Successor Activity

The activities which can not be accomplished until an activity has occurred are termed as successor.

(vi) Dummy Activity

Two or more activity which have the same head and tail events. It means that two or more activities share the same start and finish nodes simultaneously. Or we can say that an activity which only determines the dependency of one activity over the other, but does not consume any time is called a dummy activity. Dummies are usually represented by dotted lines arrows.

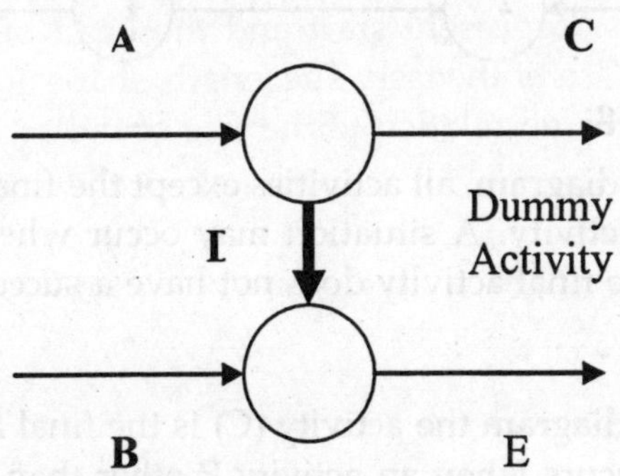

(vii) Network Diagram

A network diagram is the graphical representation of logically and sequentially connected arrows representing.

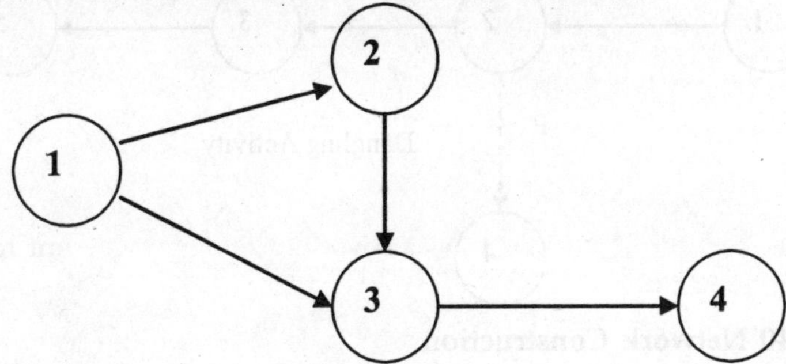

(viii) Looping

Looping is also known as cycling error. Due to error in network logic, a situation of looping occurs in which no activity can be completed as all the activities of the network are interlinked. In such situation, there is need to reexamine the network logic and redraw the network.

For Example:-The activities D, E and F form a loop. Activity D can not start until F is complete which in turn depends upon the completion of E. But E is dependent upon the completion of D

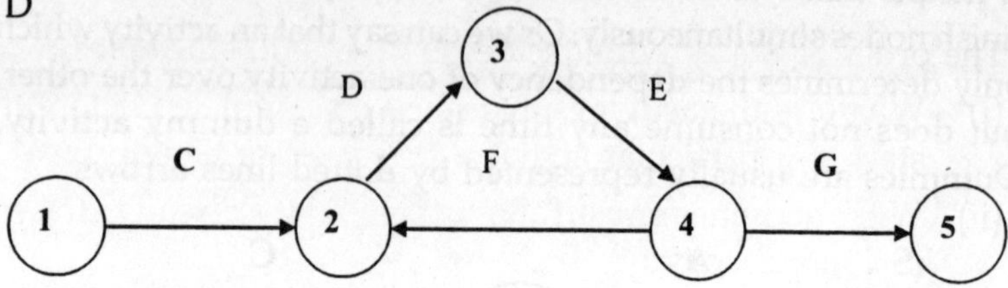

(ix) Dangling:

In a network diagram, all activities except the final activity has a successor activity. A situation may occur when an activity other than the final activity does not have a successor activity.

For Example: -

In following diagram the activity (C) is the final activity. Here a situation occurs when an activity P other than final activity (C), does not has a successor activity. So activity P is dangling activity.

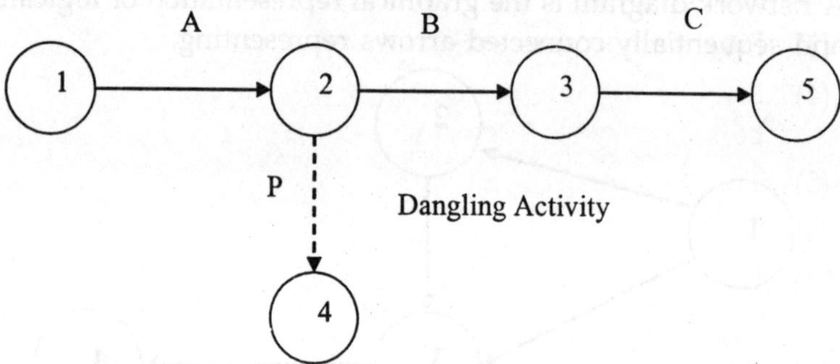

12.10 Network Construction

Network construction is a simple procedure by which all the events and activities are in logical and sequential manner to meet the requirement of a particular project. The following steps are helpful in network construction.

1) Divide the project into activities.
2) Decide the start event, the end event of project for all the

activities.

3) The activities decided by the pre-determined order are put in a logical sequence by using the graphical notation.

The order of the activity decided by the following rules:

(i) What are the activities that must be completed before the start of a particular activity? (Predecessor activity)

(ii) What activities must follow the activity already drawn? (Successor activity)

(iii) Are there any activities which must be performed simultaneously with a particular activity?

12.11 Rules of Network Construction

There are the following rules of Network construction which is given below.

(1) Activities are represented by arrows ⟶ and events are represented by circle ◯ :

(2) Each activity is represented by one and only one arrow. The tail of the arrow represents the start and head of the arrow represent end of the activity.

(3) Each activity must start and end in a node.

(4) Each arrow activity must be kept straight and should not be shown curved or bent.

(5) Try to avoid arrows which cross each other.

(6) There must be no loops.

(7) Use arrows from left to right. Avoid mixing two directions, vertical and standing arrows may be used if necessary.

(8) All events (nodes) should be numbered in an ascending order.

(9) No events numbers can be repeated.

(10) Dangling is not permitted.

12.12 Examples of Network construction

Example. 1 Construct a Network for the Project whose activities and their precedence relationship are as given below.

Activities	A	B	C	D	E	F	G	H	I
Immediate predecessor	-	-	A	A	D	B,C E	F	D	G,H

Solution: From the given table, it is clear that A and B are the beginning activity and I are the last or terminal. C, D are the beginning with the same event (A) and D is the predecessor of the activity E and H. B. E. C is the predecessor of the activity F.

F, and F has to be the predecessor of G. G and H are the predecessor of I. Thus the final Network diagram is given below.

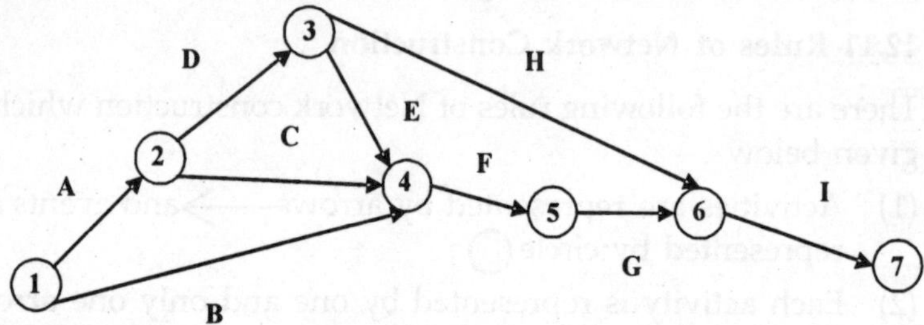

Example 2. Draw a network diagram with the help of the following table:

Activity	A	B	C	D	E	F
Predecessor	-	A	-	B,C	C	D,E

Solution: From the table it is clear that A and C are the starting activity and F is the terminal activity. In this table, it is also clear that A is the immediate predecessor of activity B. B is the predecessor of the activity D. C is the predecessor of the D and E. D, E is predecessor of activity F. So we have to introduce a dummy activity which starts at activity E to F.

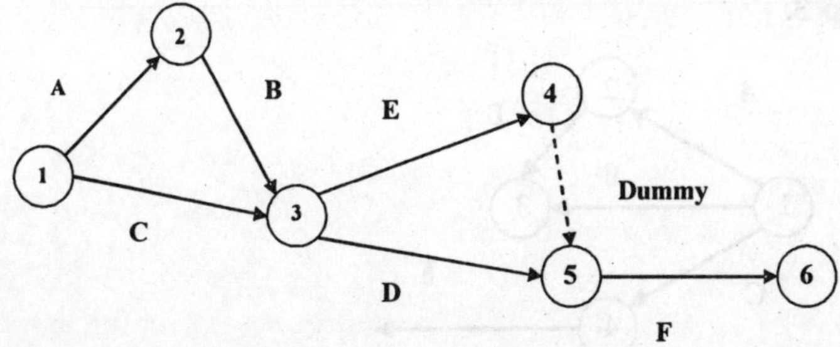

Example. 3 A, B, C can start simultaneously A<D, I; B<G, F; C<E; E<H, K; F< H, K; G< J; Draw the network diagram.

Solution:

Activity	A	B	C	D	E	F	G	H	I	J	K
Predecessor activity	-	-	-	A	C	B,D	B,D	E,F	A	G, H	E,F

Solution:

Step 1.

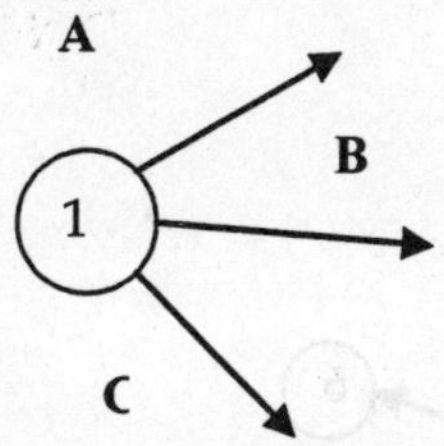

Step 2.

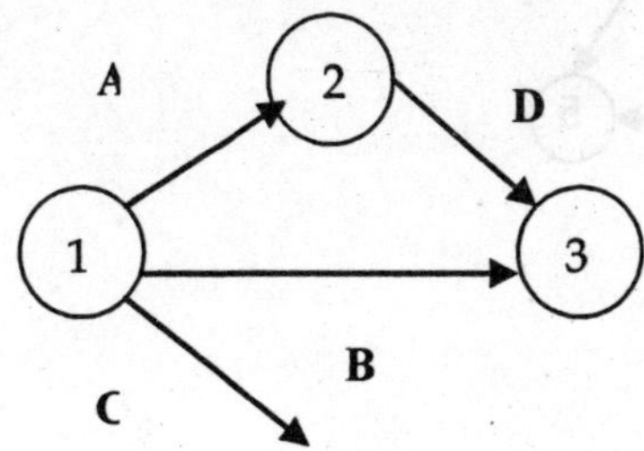

Step 3.

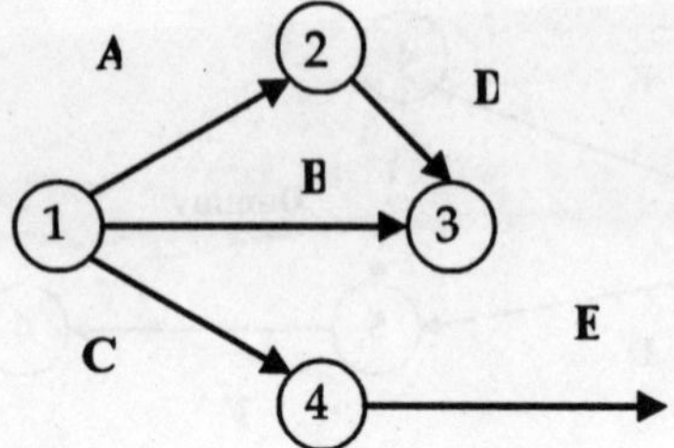

Step 4.

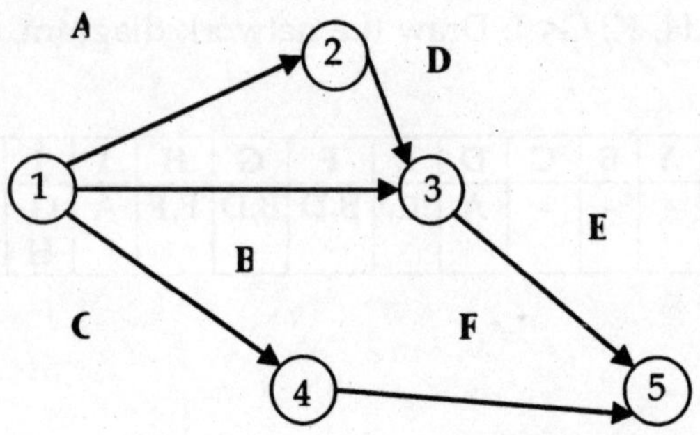

Step 5.

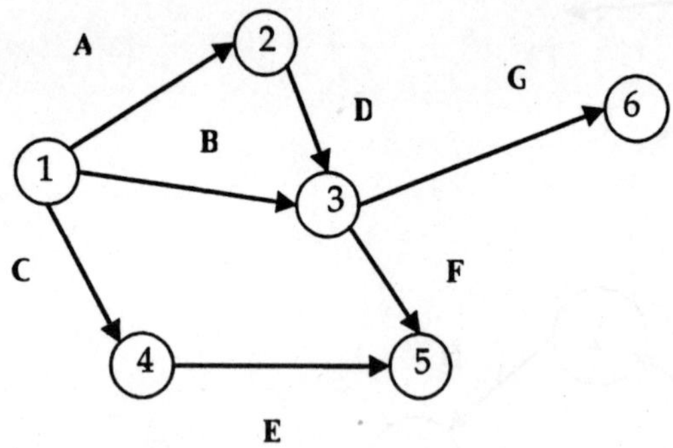

Step 6.

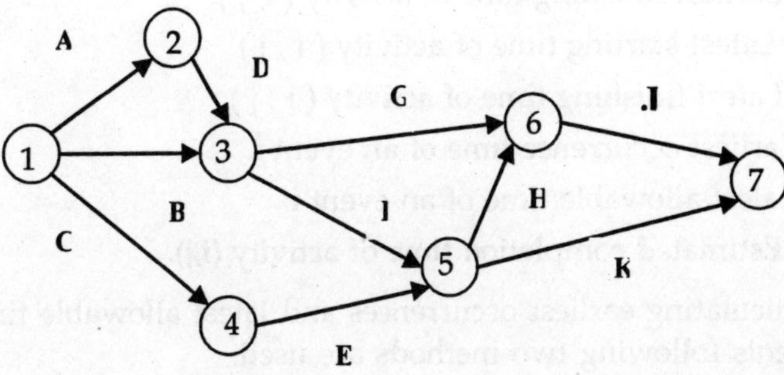

Step 7.

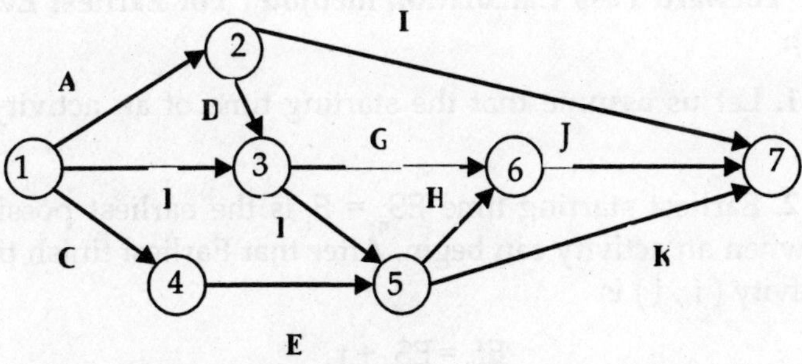

12.13 Time Analysis of Network

Time analysis of network is an important tool for the network. It is necessary for planning of various activities of the project. Without the time analysis we can't forecast the expected time take to completion of the project.

We shall use the following notation for the purpose of calculating various times of events and activities.

(i,j) = Activity (i,j) with tail event i and head event j.

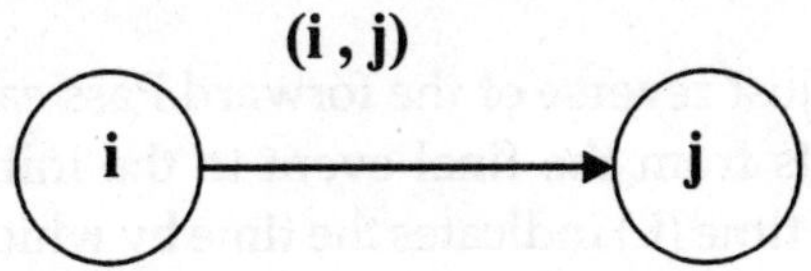

ES_{ij} = Earliest starting time of activity (i , j).

Ef_{ij} = Earliest finishing time of activity (i, j).

LS_{ij} = Latest starting time of activity (i , j).

Lf_{ij} = Latest finishing time of activity (i , j).

E_i = Earliest occurrence time of an event i.

L_i = Latest allowable time of an event i.

T_{ij} = Estimated completion time of activity (i,j).

For calculating earliest occurrences and latest allowable times of events following two methods are used.

(1) Forward Pass Calculation Method

(2) Backward Pass Calculation Method

12.14 Forward Pass Calculation method (For Earliest Event Time):

Step 1. Let us assume that the starting time of an activity is zero.

Step 2. Earliest starting time $ES_{ij} = E_i$ is the earliest possible time when an activity can begin. After that Earliest finish time of activity (i , j) is

$$Ef_{ij} = ES_{ij} + t_{ij}$$

Step 3. Earliest event time for the event (j) is the maximum of the earliest finish time of all the activities ending at that event

$$E_i = \underset{i}{\text{Max}} (E_i + t_{ij})$$

Step 4. If j = N (final event) then earliest finish time for the project, i.e the earliest occurrence time $E_N = \underset{i}{\text{Max}} \{ E_{N-1} + t_{ij} \}$ for all terminal activities.

12.15 Backward Pass Calculation (For Latest allowable Event Time):

This method is just reverse of the forward Pass calculation. The calculation starts from the final event to the initial event. The latest allowable time (L) indicates the time by which all activities entering into that event must be completed without delaying the completion of the project.

Step 1. Let assume that the ending event (E = L)

Step 2. Latest finish time (Lf_{ij}) for activity (i,j) is the target time for completing the project.

$$Lf_{ij} = L_j$$

Step 3. Latest starting time of the activity (I, j)= latest completion time of (i, j) – the activity time

$$LS_{ij} = Lf_{ij} - t_{ij}$$
$$= L_j - t_{ij}$$

Step 4. Latest event time for event (i) is the minimum of the latest strat time of all activities originating from the event

$$L_i = \underset{J}{\text{Min}} \; (L_j - t_{ij})$$

Step 5. If i = N (First event) then the latest event time for the project i.e. latest allowable time $L_1 = \underset{1}{\text{Min}} \{L_{N-1} - t_{ij}\}$ for all activities.

Floats and Slack Times:

The difference between the latest and the earliest **activity** time is known as float and the difference between the latest and the earliest **event** time is known as **slack.**

Thus the basic difference between the slack and float is that, a slack is used for events only; whereas float is used for activities only.

There are mainly three kinds of floats as given below:

Total Float: - It is the difference between maximum time available and the actual time required to perform the activity.

In the language of mathematics, the total float of an activity (i , j) is the difference between the latest start time and the earliest start time of that activity.

Total float (TF)$_{ij}$ = (latest start- earliest start) for activity (i,j).

$$\textbf{i.e} \quad (TF)_{ij} = (LS)_{ij} - (ES)_{ij}$$

$$\textbf{or} \quad (TF)_{ij} = (L_j - E_i) - t_{ij}$$

Free Float (FF):- It is excess of available time over the activity time when all jobs start as early as possible. In mathematical language, the free float for activity (i,j) ,denoted by (Ff_{ij}) can be calculated by the formula

$(Ff)_{ij}$ = Total float – Head event slack

= TF – Head event slack

Head event slack of an activity

$A = L_j - E_j$

$= 18 - 10$

$= 8$

E = 10
L = 18

i → j

Independent Float (IF):- It is the excess of minimum available time over the required activity duration.

IF_{ij} = Free float – Tail event slack

= Ff – Tail event slack

Tail event slack of activity A = $L_i - E_i$

$= 20 - 18$

$= 2$

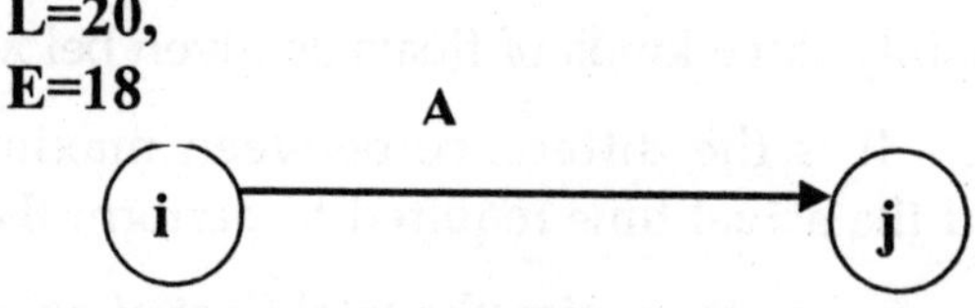

The negative independent float is always taken as zero.

Note:

1. There are following relation in between these floats.

$$IF_{ij} \leq FF_{ij} \leq TF_{ij}$$

2. If the total float (TF_{ij}) for any activity is zero then those activities are called critical activities.

12.16 Network Techniques:

There are two techniques of network analysis are critical path method (CPM) and Project Evaluation and Review Techniques (PERT).

(1) Critical Path Method (CPM):

The objective of **CPM** is to estimate the total project duration and to assign starting and finishing times to all activities involving in the project. This help on finding actual duration against the scheduled duration of the project. For Project scheduling we should know the following factors.

(i) Total completion time of the project.

(ii) Earlier and latest start time of each activity.

(iii) Float for each activity.

(iv) Critical activities and critical path.

There are the following procedures for determining the critical path is as follows.

Step 1. Construct a Network diagram.

Step 2. Locate the normal time (t_{ij}) for each activity (i,j) above the arrow which is deterministic.

Step 3. Calculate Earliest start time (E_i) and Earliest finish time for each event (i). Also calculate the latest finish time and latest start time for each event (j) and write the latest time Lj for each event j.

Step 4. Locate various times namely normal time, earliest time and latest time on the arrow diagram.

Step 5. Determine the total float for each activity by taking the difference between the earliest start and the latest start time.

Step 6. Identify critical activity and then draw critical path.

Step 7. Calculate the total project duration.

Example 1. Consider the following schedule of activities and related information for construction of a new plant.

Activity	1-2	2-3	3-6	2-4	1-5	5-6	4-6	5-7	7-8	6-8
Expected time in months	4	2	6	6	2	8	9	7	10	1

Construct the network diagram and

(a) Calculate the Critical Path

(b) Expected time to build the plant.

Solution:

(a)

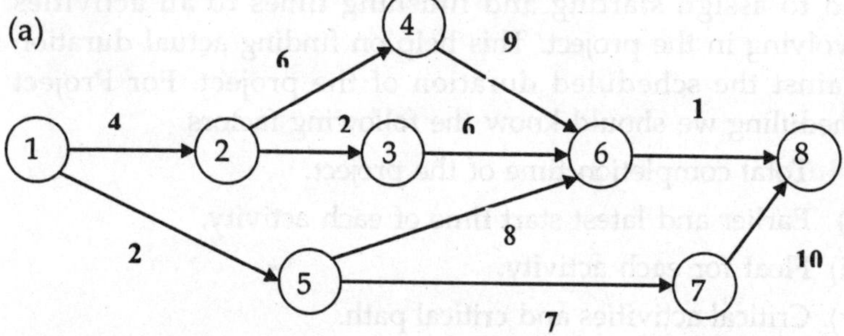

From the above network diagram, there is various number of paths from starts event (1) to finish event (8). The duration of each path can be found by adding the duration of the activities lying on those paths. Thus, we get different durations along with different paths.

Path	Duration (Months)
1-2-4-6-8	4+6+9+1=20 (Maximum)
1-2-3-6-8	4+2+6+1=13
1-5-6-8	2+8+1=11
1-5-7-8	2+7+10=19

Among the various paths, there is only one path that takes longest duration. That is called Critical Path. Hence 1-2-4-6-8 is the **critical path.**

Expected time to build the plant = The duration of the completion of the project = **20 months.**

Example 2. A project schedule has the following characteristics:

Activity	1-2	2-5	1-3	1-4	3-5	4-6	5-6
Duration (In day's)	8	10	4	6	6	8	4

From the above information, you are required to -

(1) Construct a Network diagram.

(2) Compute Earliest and Latest time for each event.

(3) Determine the Critical path and total project duration.

(4) Calculate Total, free float for each activity.

Solution:-

(1)

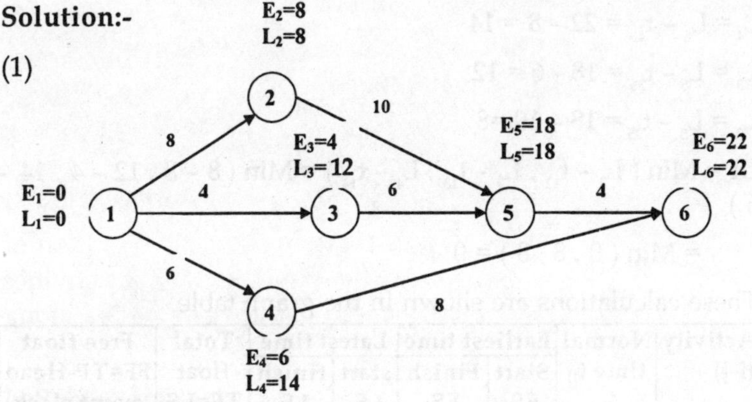

(3) The earliest and latest calculation is given below.

Forward pass calculation:

With the help of forward pass calculation, we estimate the earliest start (ES_i)

(Earliest start of event i) E_i = Max ($ES_i + t_{ij}$)

$E_1 = ES_1 = 0$

$E_2 = ES_1 + t_{12} = 0+8=8$

$E_3 = ES_1 + t_{13} = 0+4=4$

$E_4 = ES_1 + t_{14} = 0+6=6$

$E_5 = \text{Max}\ (E_2+t_{25}\ , E_3+t_{35})$

$= \text{Max}\ (8+10, 4+6)= 18$

$E_6 = \text{Max}\ (E_5+t_{56}\ , E_4+t_{46}\ )$

$= \text{Max}\ (18+4\ , 6+8) =22$

Backward Pass calculation:

With the help of backward pass calculation, we estimate the latest finish time of each event.

$L_j = \underset{j}{\text{Min}} \quad (LF_j - t_{ij})$

$L_6 = 22$

$L_5 = L_6 - t_{56} = 22 - 4 = 18$

$L_4 = L_6 - t_{46} = 22 - 8 = 14$

$L_3 = L_5 - t_{35} = 18 - 6 = 12$

$L_2 = L_5 - t_{25} = 18 - 10 =8$

L1 = $\text{Min}\ (L_2 - t_{12}\ , L_3 - t_{13}\ , L_4 - t_{14}) = \text{Min}\ (8 - 8\ , 12 - 4\ , 14 - 6\ )$

$= \text{Min}\ (0\ , 8\ , 8\ ) = 0$

These calculations are shown in the graph table.

Activity (i-j)	Normal time t_{ij}	Earliest time		Latest time		Total float TF=LS -ES	Free float FF=TF-Head event slack FF=TF-(LS_j-ES_j)
		Start ES_i	Finish ES_j	start LS_i	finish LS_j		
1-2	8	0	8	0	8	0-0=0	0-(8-8)=0
2-5	10	8	18	8	18	8-8=0	0-(18-18)=0
1-3	4	0	4	8	12	8-0=8	8-(12-4)=0
1-4	6	0	6	8	14	8-0=8	8-(14-6)=0
3-5	6	4	10	12	18	12-4=8	8-(18-10)=0
4-6	8	6	14	14	22	14-6=8	8-(22-14)=0
5-6	4	18	22	18	22	18-18=0	0-(22-22)=0

From the above table, we observe that activities 1-2,2-5, and 5-6 are the critical activities. Hence, the critical path is 1-2-5-6. Thus, the total project duration =22 day's.

Example 3. A project consist of a series of tasks labeled A,B,.......H,I; A<D,E; C<G B<F, H, D<F,G<I The notation X<Y means that the task X must be completed before Y is started.

Draw a graph to represent the sequence of tasks and find the minimum time of completion of the project, when the time (in day's) of completion of each task is as follows:

Task	A	B	C	D	E	F	G	H	I
Time (day's)	23	8	20	16	24	18	19	4	10

Solution: The given constraints can be given in the following table:

Activity	A	B	C	D	E	F	G	H	I
Preceding activity	-	-	-	A	A	B,D	C	B	F,G
Time (day's)	23	8	20	16	24	18	19	4	10

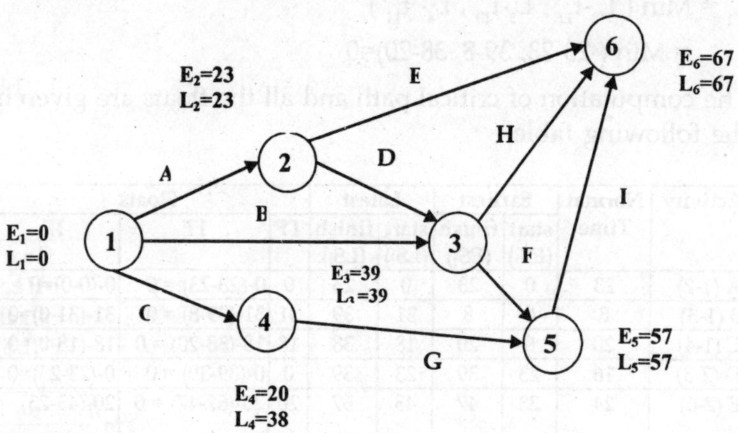

Forward pass calculation:

With the help of forward pass calculation, we estimate the earliest start time (ES_i).

Earliest start time of event (i) = E_i = Max ($ES_i + t_{ij}$)

$E_1 = 0$

$E_2 = E_1 + t_{12} = 0+23=23$

$E_3 = Max(E_1 + t_{13}, E_2 + t_{23}) = Max(0+8, 23+16) = 39$

$E_4 = E_1 + t_{14} = 0+20=20$

$E_5 = Max(E_4 + t_{45}, E_3 + t_{35}) = Max(20+19, 39+18) = 57$

$E_6 = Max(E_2 + t_{26}, E_3 + t_{36}, E_5 + t_{56}) = Max(23+24, 39+4, 57+10) = 67$

Backward pass calculation:

With the help of backward pass calculation, we estimate the latest finish time (LS_j).

$L_j = Min(LS_j - t_{ij})$

$L_6 = 67$

$L_5 = L_6 - t_{56} = 67-10=57$

$L_4 = L_5 - t_{45} = 57-19=38$

$L_3 = Min(L_6 - t_{36}, L_5 - t_{35}) = Min(67-4, 57-18)=39$

$L2 = Min(L_3 - t_{13}, L_6 - t_{26}) = Min(39-16, 67-24) = 0$

$L_1 = Min(L_2 - t_{12}, L_3 - t_{13}, L_4 - t_{14})$

$= Min(23-23, 39-8, 38-20)=0$

The computation of critical path and all the floats are given in the following table:

Activity	Normal Time	Earliest		Latest		Floats		
		start (ES_i)	finish (ES_j)	start (LS_i)	finish (LS_j)	TF	FF	IF
A (1-2)	23	0	23	0	23	0	0-(23-23) = 0	0-(0-0)=0
B (1-3)	8	0	8	31	39	31	31-(39-8) = 0	31-(31-0)=0
C (1-4)	20	0	20	18	38	18	18-(38-20) = 0	18-(18-0)=0
D (2-3)	16	23	39	23	39	0	0-(39-39) = 0	0-(23-23)=0
E (2-6)	24	23	47	43	67	20	20-(67-47) = 0	20-(43-23) = 0
F (3-5)	18	39	57	39	57	0	0-(57-57) = 0	0-(39-39)=0
G (4-5)	19	20	39	38	57	18	18-(57-39) = 0	18-(38-20)=0
H (3-6)	4	39	43	63	67	24	24-(67-43) = 0	24-(63-39) = 0
I (5-6)	10	57	67	57	67	0	0-(67-67) = 0	0-(57-57)=0

The above table shows that the critical activity are 1-2 , 2-3 ,3-5 and 5-6 as their total float is zero. Hence, we have the critical path= 1-2-3-5-6.

Total project duration = 67 day's.

Advantages of CPM:

1. It helps in ascertaining time schedules of project.
2. It identifies most critical activities.
3. With the help of CPM better and detailed planning is possible.
4. Management control becomes easy.
5. It helps management in diverting resources from non-critical activity to critical activities.
6. It is helpful for determining the sequence of jobs and earliest completion date for the project.
7. It is also helpful for better utilization of resources.

(2) Project Evaluation Method (PERT):

CPM is based on the assumption that the times, with each activity in the project will take it precise and known. However, in real life project various activities are based on judgment. It is difficult to obtain a reliable time estimate due to the changing technology. Thus, we can say that estimated activity time in CPM is deterministic in nature. For such cases where the activities are non-deterministic in nature, PERT was developed.

Hence PERT is a probabistic method where the activity times are represented by a probability distribution. PERT has three time estimates. Thus, probability distribution of activity times is based upon three different time estimates made for each activity. These are given as

(i) Optimistic time estimate (t_o or a)

(ii) Most likely time estimate (t_m or m)

(iii) Pessimistic time estimate (t_p or b)

Optimistic time estimate (t_o or a) = It is the smallest time taken to complete the activity if everything goes on well. (It has rarely occurs).

Most likely time estimate (t_m or m) = it refers to the estimate of the normal time the activity would take. (It has normally occurs).

Pessimistic time estimate = It is the longest time that an activity would take if every thing goes wrong.

The time distribution curves of three time estimates are as given below. We have to calculate the expected time of an activity. It is given by the weighted average of the three time estimates.

Expected time of an activity = $(t_0 + 4\,t_m + t_p) / 6$

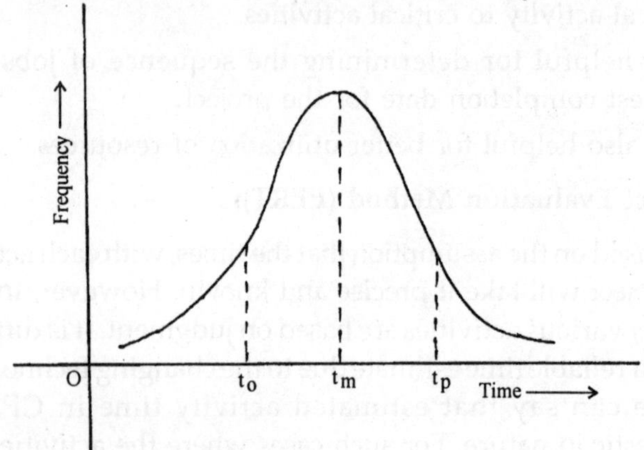

Note : It is given by the help of â distribution with weight of 1, 4 ,1 for t_0 , t_m , t_p.

Variance of the activity is given by

$$\sigma^2 = \left(\frac{t_p - t_0}{6}\right)^2$$

The main objective of PERT is to find the completion for a particular event within specified date T_s given by P $(Z \leq D)$

$$Z^2 = \frac{T_s - T_e}{\sigma}$$

Where T_s = Scheduled time to complete the project

σ = Expected Standard deviation of the project length.

T_e = normal expected project length duration.

PERT procedure

Step 1. Construct the network diagram.

Step 2. Calculate the expected duration of each activity

Also calculate the expected variance of each activity.

Step 3. Calculate earliest start (ES), earliest finish (EF), latest start (LS), latest finish (LF) and total float of each activity.

Step 4. Finds the critical path and identifies the critical activities.

Step 5. Calculate the standard normal variable. Using the normal curve are estimate the probability of completing the project within a specified time.

Example: - The following table lists the jobs of a network with their estimates.

Job (i-j)	Expected Duration(day's)		
	Optimistic (to)	Most Likely (tm)	Pessimistic (tp)
(1-2)	3	6	15
(1-6)	2	5	14
(2-3)	6	12	30
(2-4)	2	5	8
(3-5)	5	11	17
(4-5)	3	6	15
(6-7)	3	9	27
(5-8)	1	4	7
(7-8)	4	19	28

(a) Draw the project network.

(b) Calculate the length and variance of the critical path, and

(c) What is the approximate probability that the jobs on the critical path will be completed in 41 days?

Solution: - Using the formula

t_e = (to +4 tm +tp) / 6and σ^2 = {(tp – to) / 6 } ^{2} we have to calculate te and σ^2.

Activity	Estimated Time			σ	te	Earliest		Latest		TF
	to	tm	tp			Start	Finish	Start	Finish	
1-2	3	6	15	4	7	0	7	0	7	0
1-6	2	5	14	4	6	0	6	1	7	1
2-3	6	12	30	16	14	7	21	7	21	0
2-4	2	5	8	1	5	7	12	20	25	13
3-5	5	11	17	4	11	21	32	21	32	0
4-5	3	6	15	4	7	12	19	25	32	13
6-7	3	9	27	16	11	6	17	7	18	1
5-8	1	4	7	1	4	32	36	32	36	0
7-8	4	19	28	16	18	17	25	18	36	1

Forward Pass Calculation

The earliest expected times are calculated as-

$E_1=0$

$E_2= E_1+ t_{12} = 0+7=7$

$E_3=E_2+ t_{23} =7+14=21$

$E_4=E_3+t_{24} =7+5=12$

$E_5=\text{Max} [E_4+t_{45} , E_3+t_{35}]=\text{Max} [12+7 , 21+11]=32$

$E_6=E_1+t_{16}=0+6=6$

$E_7=E_6+t_{67}=6+11=17$

$E_8=\text{Max} [E_7+t_{78} , E_5+t_{58}]=\text{Max} [17+18,32+4]$

$=\text{Max} [35,36]=36$

Backward Pass calculation

The Latest expected times are calculated as

$L_8=36$

$L_7=L_8 - t_{78} = 36 - 18 = 18$

$L_6 = L_7 - t_{67} = 18-11=7$

$L_5 = L_8 - t_{58} = 36 - 4 = 32$

$L_4 = L_5 - t_{45} = 32 - 7 = 25$

$L_3 = L_5 - t_{35} = 32 - 11 = 21$

$L_2 = \text{Min} [L_4 - t_{24} , L_3 - t_{23}] = \text{Min} [25 - 5 , 21 - 14] = 7$

$L_1 = \text{Min} [L_2 - t_{12} , L_6 - t_{16}] = \text{Min} [7 - 7 , 7 - 6] = 0$

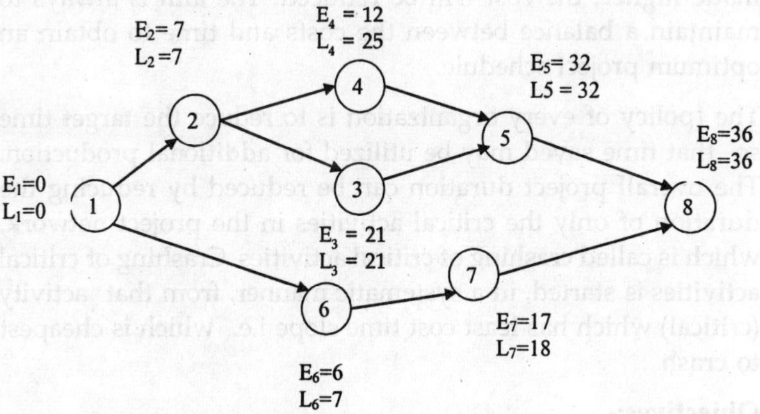

From the above table critical path is 1-2-3-5-8 .

The optimum length of the critical path is 36 days.

Variance of the critical path = 4 + 16 + 4 + 1= 25

Now the schedule time of completing the jobs is given 41 days. Therefore, the distance in standard deviations, that schedule time for earliest expected time is given by

$$D = \frac{T_s - T_e}{\sigma} = \frac{T_s - T_e}{\sigma} = \frac{41 - 46}{\sigma} = \frac{5}{5} = 1$$

Hence $P (z \leq D) = 0.84$ which is area under standard normal curve bounded by the ordinates X = 0 and X = 1

This concludes that only 16 times the job would take time longer than 41 days.

12.17 Project Crashing:

The objective of the CPM and PERT is to compute the optimum duration of the projects completion. But time is related to cost and the objective is to develop an optimum time cost relationship.

Many times it becomes necessary to complete the project earlier than the normal time. Generally, the cost of the project goes up if the project time is reduced. Similarly, if the duration of is made higher, the cost will be reduced. The aim is always to maintain a balance between the costs and time to obtain an optimum project schedule.

The [policy of every organization is to reduce the target time so that time saved may be utilized for additional production. The overall project duration can be reduced by reducing the duration of only the critical activities in the project network, which is called crashing of critical activities. Crashing of critical activities is started, in a systematic manner, from that activity (critical) which has least cost time slope i.e. which is cheapest to crash.

Objectives:-

1. To reduce the normal duration of the project at minimum extra cost.
2. To maintain a balance between time and cost to obtain an optimum project scheduled.
3. To save the time and resources for allocation of more profitable activities.

Terms used in Crashing:

Normal Cost (NC): It is the lowest cost of completing the activity in the minimum time. Normal means not using overtime or other additional resources.

Normal Time (NT): It is the minimum time required to achieve the project with normal cost.

Crash Cost (CC): It is the lest cost of completing an activity using all possible means like overtime, additional machinery etc.

$$\text{Cost slope} = \frac{(\text{Crash Cost} - \text{Normal Cost})}{(\text{Normal Time} - \text{Crash Time})}$$

Crash Time (CT): It is absolute minimum time associated with crash cost.

Project Crashing Example:

Example 1: Table below shows, jobs and their normal time and cost and crash time and cost for a project.

Activity	1 – 2	1 – 3	2 – 3	2 – 4	3 – 4	3 – 5	4 – 6	5 – 6
Normal Time	6	8	4	3	0	6	10	3
Normal cost	1400	1200	1100	800	-	900	2500	500
Crash Time	4	5	2	2	-	3	6	2
Crash Cost	1900	2800	1500	1400	-	1600	3500	800

Indirect cost for the Project is Rs 300 per day.

1. Draw the network of the project.
2. What is normal duration and cost of the project?
3. If all activities are crashed, what will be the project duration and crash cost?
4. Find the optimum duration and minimum project cost ?

Solution:

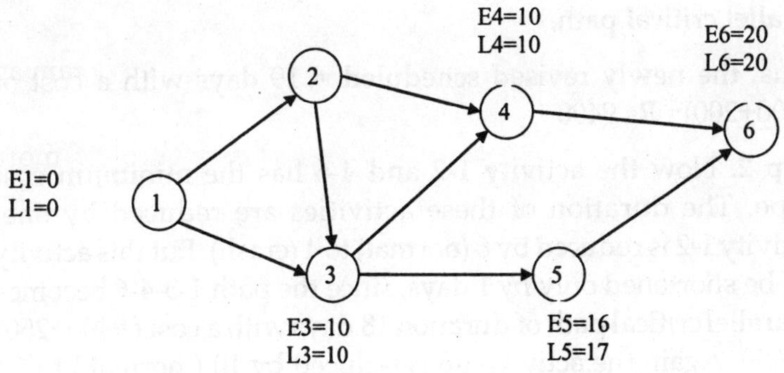

Critical Paths

Paths	Durations(days)
1-2-4-6	6+3+10=19
1-2-3-5-6	6+4+6+3=19
1-2-3-4-6	6+4+0+10=20
1-3-5-6	8+6+3=17
1-3-4-6	8+0+10=18

So the longest duration is 20 is a critical path i.e 1-2-3-4-6

The normal time = 20 days

The normal cost = 1400+2000+1100+800+0+900+2500+500=Rs 9200

Now calculate the different minimum cost schedule which can occur between normal and crash times mainly depending on the time slopes for the different activities.

Activity	1-2	1-3	2-3	2-4	3-5	4-6	5-6
Slope	250	267	200	600	233	250	300

Existing schedule involves more time; the schedule is reduced by crashing some of the activities.

Step 1. the activity 2-3 has the minimum cost slope. The duration of this activity is reduced by 4 (normal) to 2 (crash) days.

Cost of crashing = 2 × 200 = 400 but this activity should be shortened only by one day, since this path 1-2-4-6 becomes a parallel critical path.

Thus, the newly revised scheduled = 19 days with a cost of (9200+200)= Rs 9400

Step 2. Now the activity 1-2 and 4-6 has the minimum cost slope. The duration of these activities are reduced by one. Activity 1-2 is reduced by 6 (normal) to 4 (crash). But this activity can be shortened only by 1 days, since the path 1-3-4-6 becomes a parallel critical path of duration 18 days with a cost (9400+250) = 9650. Again the activity 4-6 is reduced by 10 (normal) to 6 (crash) but this activity can be shortened only by 1 days, since this path 1-3-5-6 becomes a parallel critical path of duration 17 days with cost (9650 +2500) = Rs 9900.

Calculation of minimum total cost

	Normal Project Duration (days)	**Crashing time and cost (Rs)**	**Indirect cost (Rs)**	**Total cost (Rs)**
1	20	-	20 × 300 =600	600
2	19	1×200	19 × 300=5700	5700+200=5650
3	18	1×250	18 × 300=5400	5400+250=5650
4	17	1×250	17 × 300=5100	5100+250=5350
5	16	1×200+1×600+1× 233 =1033	16 × 300=4800	4800+1033=5833

Therefore, from the table, the minimum total cost is Rs 5350 and the optimum duration of the project is 17 days.

12.18 Practice Problem:

1. The objective of network analysis is
   (i) To minimize total project duration.
   (ii) To minimize total project cost
   (iii) To minimize production delays, interruption and conflicts.
   (iv) All of the above

2. The advantage of network models in
   (i) Project planning
   (ii) Project scheduling
   (iii) Project controlling
   (iv) All of the above

3. Activity Slack time is also represented by
   (i) total float
   (ii) free float
   (iii) independent float
   (iv) all of the above

Generally PERT techniques is useful for the project of
(i) repetitive nature
(ii) non-repetitive nature
(iii) deterministic nature
(iv) non of the above

The slack can be calculated by
(i) LF - LS
(ii) EF - ES
(iii) LS - ES
(iv) All of the above

If an activity has zero slack, it implies that
(i) It lies on the critical path
(ii) It is a dummy activity
(iii) The project is processing well
(iv) None of the above

A dummy activity is used in the network diagram when
(i) two parallel activities have the same tail and head events
(ii) the chain of activities may have common event yet be independent by them selves
(iii) both (i) and (ii)
(iv) None of the above

In PERT the range of time between the optimistic and pessimistic time estimates of an activity is
(i) 3 ó
(ii) 6 ó
(iii) 12 ó
(iv) None of the above

PERT stands for
(i) Programme Evaluation and Review Technique
(ii) Project Evaluation and Review Technique
(iii) Product Evaluated and Review Technique
(iv) Process Evaluation and Review Technique

CPM was developed by
(i) E. I . DuPont

(ii) Jon Von Neuman
(iii) Morse & Kimball
(iv) George Dantzig

11. In time cost –trade-off function analysis
    (i) Cost decreases linearly as time increases
    (ii) Cost at normal time is zero
    (iii) Cost increases linearly as time increases
    (iv) None of the above

12. The activity which can be delayed without affecting the execution of the immediate succeeding activity determined by
    (i) total float
    (ii) free float
    (iii) independent float
    (iv) none of the above

Answer: 1. (i) , 2. (iv) , 3.(iv) , 4. (iv) , 5. (iii), 6. (i) , 7. (iii) , 8. (ii), 9. (i) , 10. (i) , 11. (i) , 12. (ii) .

1. What is Project Management?
2. What is Project Cycle?
3. What are the objectives of Network Analysis?
4. Explain the function of project management?
5. What do you mean by CPM ?
6. What is PERT?
7. What are the rules of Network Construction?
8. What are the basic terms which are used in Network Analysis?
9. What are the causes of delay in Project Management?
10. What are the limitations of Network analysis?
11. What are the advantages of Network analysis?
12. Write the short notes on following
    (i) Time Analysis
    (ii) Forward Pass calculation
    (iii) Backward Pas calculation
    (iv) Floats

(v) Slack
(vi) Dummy activity
(vii) Cost slope
(viii)Project cost
(ix) Project Crashing

8. The following table shows the jobs of a network along with their time estimates.

Job	1-2	1-6	2-3	2-4	3-5	4-5	6-7	5-8	7-8
a(days)	1	2	2	2	7	5	5	3	8
m	7	5	14	5	10	5	8	3	17
b	13	14	26	8	19	17	29	9	32

Draw the project network and find the probability that the project is completed in 40 days.

Activity	Estimated Duration (weeks)		
	Optimistic (a)	Most likely(m)	Pessimistic(b)
1-2	1	1	7
1-3	1	4	7
2-4	2	2	8
2-5	1	1	1
3-5	2	5	14
4-6	2	5	8
5-6	3	6	15

(a) Draw the project Network
(b) Find the expected duration and variance for each activity. What is the expected project length?
(c) Calculate the variance and standard deviation of the project length. What is the probability that the project will be completed?
(d) If the project due date is 19 weeks, what is the probability of not meeting the due date:

Given : 0.5 0.67 1.00 1.33 2.00

Probability : 0.3085 0.2514 0.1587 0.0918 0.0228

10. A project schedule has the following characteristics.

Activity	Time	Activity	Time
1-2	4	5-6	4
1-3	1	5-7	8
2-4	1	6-8	1
3-4	1	7-8	2
3-5	6	8-10	5
4-9	5	9-10	7

(i) Construct a PERT network.
(ii) Compute T_E and T_L for each event.
(iii) Find the critical path.
(iv) Also obtain the total and free floats for each activity.

11. A project plan is as follows:

Activity	Predecessors	Time	Activity	Predecessors	Time
A	—	8	G	E	6
B	—	2	H	E	3
C	A	1	I	G	3
D	B	9	J	H	5
E	B	4	K	I.J	2
F	C,D	5	L	F	3

Construct a Network and compute the early start, late start and slack ime for each activity. Indicate the critical path.

13. A project plan is as follows:

Activity	Predecessors	Time
A	—	5
B	A	7
C	B	2
D	B	3
E	C	1
F	D	2
G	C	1
H	E,F	3
I	G,H	10

(i) Draw a critical path scheduling arrow diagram, identifying jobs by letters and associated time each. Indicate critical path.

(ii) What is the minimum time for completion of the project?

14. For a small project of 12 activities, the details are given below. Draw the network and find earliest occurrence time, latest occurrence time, critical activities and project completion time.

Activity	A	B	C	D	E	F	G	H	I	J	K	L
Dependence	—	—	—	B.C	A	C	E	E	D,F,H	E	I,J	G
Duration (days)	9	4	7	8	7	5	10	8	6	9	10	2

15. A building construction project has the following time schedule .

Activity	Time in Months	Activity	Time in months
1-2	2	4-6	3
1-3	2	5-8	1
1-4	1	6-9	5
2-5	4	7-8	4
3-6	8	8-9	3
3-7	5		

(i) Construct network diagram

(ii) Compare total float for each activity

(iii) Critical path and its duration

16. A project is represented by the network shown below and has the following data.

Task	A	B	C	D	E	F	G	H	I
Optimistic time:	5	18	26	16	15	6	7	7	3
Pessimistic time:	10	22	40	20	25	12	12	9	5
Most likely time:	8	20	33	18	20	9	10	8	4

Determine the following.

(a) Expected task times and their variances.

(b) The earliest and latest expected times to reach each event.

(c) The critical path.

(d) The probability of an event occurring at the proposed completion date, if the original contract time of completing the project is 41.5 weeks.

17. The owner of a chain of fast food restaurants is considering new computer system for accounting and inventory control. A computer company sent the following information about the computer system installation.

Activity	Immediate Predecessor	Estimated Duration (weeks)		
		Optimistic (a)	Most likely (m)	Pessimistic(b)
A	—	4	6	8
B	A	5	7	15
C	A	4	8	12
D	B	15	20	25
E	B	10	18	26
F	C	8	9	16
G	E	4	8	12
H	D,F	1	2	3
I	G,I	6	7	8

(i) Construct an arrow diagram for this problem.

(ii) Determine the critical path and compute the expected completion time

(iii) Determine the probability of completing the project in 55 days.

18. The following table gives data on normal time and cost and crash time and cost for a project.

Activity	Normal		Crash	
	Time (weeks)	Cost(Rs)	Time (weeks)	Cost(Rs)
1-2	3	300	2	400
2-3	3	30	3	30
2-4	7	420	5	580
2-5	9	720	7	810
3-5	5	250	4	300
4-5	0	0	0	0
5-6	6	320	4	410
6-7	4	400	3	470
6-8	13	780	10	900
7-8	10	1000	9	1200

Indirect cost is Rs 50 per week.

(i) Draw the network and identify the critical path with a double.

(ii) What are the normal project duration and associated cost?

(iii) Find out the total float associated with each activity.

(iv) Crash the relevant activities systematically and determine the optimal project completion time and cost.

19. The following is the table showing details of project.

Activity	Immediate Predecessor	Normal		Crash	
		Time	Cost (Rs'000)	Tim e	Cost (Rs'000)
A	—	10	20	7	30
B	—	8	15	6	20
C	B	5	8	4	14
D	B	6	11	4	15
E	B	8	9	5	15
F	E	5	5	4	8
G	A,D,C	12	3	8	4

Indirect cost is Rs 400 per day. Find the optimum duration and associated minimum project cost.

Index

T

U

V

Z